ROUTLEDGE LIBRARY EDITIONS:
MARRIAGE

I0127756

Volume 17

WOMEN AND
MARRIAGE IN
INDIA

WOMEN AND MARRIAGE IN INDIA

P. THOMAS

Routledge
Taylor & Francis Group

LONDON AND NEW YORK

First published in 1939 by George Allen & Unwin Ltd

This edition first published in 2023
by Routledge
4 Park Square, Milton Park, Abingdon, Oxon OX14 4RN

and by Routledge
605 Third Avenue, New York, NY 10158

Routledge is an imprint of the Taylor & Francis Group, an informa business

© 1939 P. Thomas

All rights reserved. No part of this book may be reprinted or reproduced or utilised in any form or by any electronic, mechanical, or other means, now known or hereafter invented, including photocopying and recording, or in any information storage or retrieval system, without permission in writing from the publishers.

Trademark notice: Product or corporate names may be trademarks or registered trademarks, and are used only for identification and explanation without intent to infringe.

British Library Cataloguing in Publication Data
A catalogue record for this book is available from the British Library

ISBN: 978-1-032-46071-0 (Set)
ISBN: 978-1-032-47291-1 (Volume 17) (hbk)
ISBN: 978-1-032-47294-2 (Volume 17) (pbk)
ISBN: 978-1-003-38544-8 (Volume 17) (ebk)

DOI: 10.4324/9781003385448

Publisher's Note
The publisher has gone to great lengths to ensure the quality of this reprint but points out that some imperfections in the original copies may be apparent.

Disclaimer
The publisher has made every effort to trace copyright holders and would welcome correspondence from those they have been unable to trace.

Language Disclaimer
This book is a re-issue originally published in 1939. The language used and views portrayed are a reflection of its era and no offence is meant by the Publishers to any reader by this re-publication.

WOMEN AND MARRIAGE
IN INDIA

by

P. THOMAS

LONDON
GEORGE ALLEN & UNWIN LTD
MUSEUM STREET

FIRST IMPRESSION IN 1939

ALL RIGHTS RESERVED

PRINTED IN GREAT BRITAIN
in 11-Point Fournier Type
BY UNWIN BROTHERS LIMITED
WOKING

CONTENTS

CHAPTER I

Are Marriages Made in Heaven?

★

MARRIAGE is a loose word that defies definition. It is applied indifferently to the group relations existing among certain savages as well as to the Seventh Sacrament of the Roman Catholic. Between these two extremes are various forms of marriage, some so strange that we would not regard them as marriage but for their names. The Hassayeah Arabs of the White Nile region, for example, restrict the marital rights of husbands to Monday, Tuesday, Wednesday, and Thursday, whilst the wives are at liberty on the remaining three to consort with whomsoever they please. While with all civilized people marriage is supposed largely to be an initiation to the mysteries of sex, among primitive tribes like the Caribbeans of the Mosquito Coast and the Comanches, promiscuity is the rule, and marriage a restraining institution which limits an individual's sexual rights to a definite number of persons.

Among civilized people, too, every community is a law unto itself in matters matrimonial and each holds the usages of others in great contempt. The Tibetans, again, do not marry individuals. Among them it is a marriage of families, and women of one family have conjugal rights over all the men of the other. To many African tribes and to certain hill-tribes in India the laws of matrimony are sacred, but those of hospitality are more sacred, and a wife is lent to guests and visitors. Then there are the Moi of Indo-China, of whom it is said that they seldom allow a couple to marry until the children are old enough to take part in their parents' wedding feast. Thus, Prajapati, who said one thing about marriage to Manu did not say the same thing to Moses, Mohammed, St. Paul, or to the medicine men of savage tribes and the Dalai Lama of Thibet. In fact, he contradicted himself.

Now, dismissing the inviolable sanctity of all these forms of marriage, which may be regarded as truly sacred? If we overcome the subjective tendency of defending the exclusive sanctity of the particular marriage ceremony we have ourselves undergone or out of which we have been born, and view the problem objectively, we will have to admit that none of these marriages can be taken as absolute in itself but that marriage, like all other human institutions, is a modifiable social arrangement, influenced by the varying environments obtaining in various communities. Even the same community has had different standards of sexual morality at different times.

THE SANCTITY OF MATRIMONY

Although we have been led to believe that the forces that brought about the sanctification of marriage in India were exclusively spiritual, we have reason to think that they were mainly political and economical.

1. THE POLITICAL FORCES.—If we overcome the fear of sacrilege and examine our slow-dying sacred institutions and codes critically, we will find that most of them have been iniquitous in the extreme. The Divine Right of Kings, we

know, sanctified tyranny. The Infallibility of the Pope ensured godly treatment to the Catholic clergy. The sacredness of the caste system brought about the Olympian superiority of Indo-Aryans over the aborigines, who were reduced to virtual slavery and were treated as untouchables and unapproachables. The sacred codes of Manu and Moses sought to establish the dominance of one community or caste over the rest of mankind for all time. The sanctity of the Vedas and the Bible assured an easy life to a parasitic priesthood. And the sacredness of the person of the Brahmin gave him immunity from assaults by the lower orders, be his treatment of them ever so iniquitous.

Thus, we find, that sanctity is, to a large extent, veiled iniquity. The reason for this is not far to seek. In the ancient and medieval world sanctifying an unjust institution was found to be the most effective method of enforcing it on those who stood to lose by it. In addition to the fear of the severe punishments generally attached to blasphemy and sacrilege, the very considerable forces of religious suggestion could also be brought into play in making people observe sacred laws. Moreover, the very vice of an iniquitous ordinance feared exposure by open enquiry and called for sanctified mystery. In an age of revolt, for example, when the privileges of the Brahmins founded on the authority of ancient texts began to be questioned, Manu did not establish the infallibility of the Vedas by logic as the later scholiasts tried to do, but merely promulgated a code of revealed laws which intensified the sanctity of the Sruties and Smrities, so that the profane Sudra who tried to question the sanity of a text which treated him as worse than a dog stood in danger of losing his tongue. And so long as there was the armed force of a king to drive home the point, there was never much difficulty in persuading the public that Prajapati had confided the code to Manu for the edification of mankind. The necessity for the king's army came only in the initial stages. Afterwards, observing the law became a habit with the people and went down to posterity as a sacred and profound usage.

This is how many of the most obviously iniquitous institutions have come down to us as irrevocably sacred. The laws of matrimony are no exception to this general rule; in fact, our matrimonial codes are more sacred because they are more vulnerable.

We know for a fact that the position of women among Indo-Aryans was very low in the Middle Ages and very high in Vedic times. The Mahabharata tells us of women's status in yet earlier times. In his discourse on morals, King Pandu tells his consort:

"O Kunti! What thou hast said is quite true. But I shall now tell thee the practice of old, indicated by illustrious Rishies fully acquainted with every rule of morality. Women formerly were not immured within their houses and dependent on husbands and other relatives. They used to go about freely, enjoying themselves as they wished. They did not then cling to their husbands faithfully, and yet they were not considered sinful; for that was the sanctioned custom of the times. . . . That practice sanctioned by precedent is applauded by great Rishies. The practice is yet regarded with respect among the Northern Kurus. Indeed, that custom so lenient to women has the sanction of antiquity. The present practice, however (of woman being confined to one husband for life), hath been established but lately."*

* *The Mahabharata*, translated by P. C. Roy, p. 248.

Are Marriages Made in Heaven?

This passage, according to sociologists, refers to matriarchal times in India. We have other data, too, to show that Indo-Aryan society in its most ancient form was matriarchal and that women dominated the political and social life of the community. From those remote times right up to the British period women have been gradually losing their prestige and position. Even as early as Manu's code their status was reduced to that of a chattel. Far from being "free and independent of their husbands and other male relatives," the code refers to women as unfit for independence. It also treats women as the earth and lays down elaborate instructions defining masculine rights of ownership of the earth and raising crops thereon. And this was only the beginning. Not long after the promulgation of the code, we find women mounting the funeral pyres of their husbands to keep them company in the next world.

This subjection of woman to the will of man was, like all sex-conflicts, essentially a subtle process. And marriage was the one institution which was unscrupulously used to bring about the fall of women. Its vital nature made subtle deception easy to practise and, with the taboos attached to sex itself, the sanctification of marriage was all that was required to raise the institution above all critical enquiry. Accordingly, marriage was sanctified, and this pious robe of sanctity served as a cover for many a gross iniquity.

An unmarried woman, even in medieval times, had many rights a married woman had not. But every woman, except a courtesan, had to marry at some time of her life, and with marriage she lost her individuality. "Whatever be the qualities of the man with whom a woman is united according to law, such qualities even she assumes as a river united with the ocean."* Again, "no sacrifice, no vow, no fast must be performed by women apart from their husbands; if a wife obeys her husband she will for that reason alone be exalted in heaven."†

If marriage were an understanding freely entered into by two people of equal status for the propagation of the species and for their own happiness, there would have been no necessity for its sanctification. But marriage, as it has come down to us, is an institution of sex-slavery. It is an institution by means of which the ownership of a woman is transferred from her father or guardian to her husband. While the rights of a parent over his daughter is restricted at least by the taboos of incest, those of a husband over his wife were complete and absolute. An abject slave to her owner, a married woman could not plead lack of virtue in her husband as an excuse for disloyalty, any more than a bond-slave could with regard to his owner. "Though destitute of virtue or seeking pleasure elsewhere or devoid of good qualities, yet a husband must be constantly worshipped as a god by a faithful wife."‡

The sanctity of matrimony is the sanctity of subtle tyranny. Perhaps the ancients had good grounds for sanctifying tyranny. Without tyranny they found efficient government impossible. In former days, when conceptions of law and justice were in their infancy and the authority of the State but nominal, personal relations stood for much and the best way of governing a community was thought to be by disciplining all persons through sacred codes into slavery to

* Manu ix. 22.   † Ibid., v. 155.   ‡ Ibid., v. 154.
NOTE—All quotations from Manu appearing in this book are taken from *Sacred Books of the East*, vol. xxv, edited by Max Muller.

14

social superiors. The definition of relations between man and man in a State which in theory recognizes the equality of all men is an elaborate and highly complicated affair which the ancient and medieval States were not advanced enough to put into practice. It was much easier to lay it down that the king could do what he pleased with anybody in the kingdom, the noble with anybody in his particular jurisdiction, the Zamindar in his Zamindary and the peasant and the labourer in their homes.

Sex relations, too, were defined in the same spirit. From their pastoral life Indo-Aryans gradually settled down into village communities and, hemmed in by hostile tribes, they felt the necessity for a compact, disciplined society. And in this society woman had to be the slave of man, as otherwise it was thought necessary that man should be the slave of woman. And as man is physically superior, he could always prove by his might that he is to be the master in his own house.

Sanctifying tyranny may have been suited to the conditions of our ancestors. But we to-day know of better forms of government than those founded on tyranny and it ill-behoves us to retain the sanctity of an institution which has its roots in iniquity.

2. THE ECONOMIC FORCES.—In every society, the problem of rearing the young is most vital. The main object of marriage in a patriarchal community is to define a man's economic obligation in the matter of supporting children. And only in patriarchal communities wherein this obligation is entirely paternal do we find any sanctity attached to marriage.

In matriarchal communities women are the owners of

Women and Marriage in India

wealth and the duty of supporting children devolves upon the mother and her family. The father is more or less an outsider to the family, an incident in the process of reproduction. Matrimonial ties are not sacred and marriage is more of a mating arrangement than a sacrament. In some matriarchates sex-love is casual and even frivolous. Shorn of his sacred responsibility of feeding his children, the father becomes a nonentity and sexual relations a mere biological function.

In matriarchal times among Indo-Aryans, the duty of supporting children devolved upon mothers; and marriage in those days was a very liberal institution which Pandu described as analogous to the love-making of kine. But with the subjection of women and their economic disinheritance, man became the bread-winner and the supporter of children. And this change, naturally enough, raised the vexed problem of cuckoldom. The relation between a child and its mother is direct and undisputed whereas the claim of a father to a child is indirect and even doubtful. "Maternity is a matter of observation whereas paternity is a matter of inference." And man tried to overcome this natural disability by insisting on the fidelity of his wife; an attempt, by the way, not completely successful to this day.

It should not, however, be imagined that men are incapable of loving and supporting children other than their own. Adoption apart, it must be remembered that among many savages paternity was unknown till the European missionaries enlightened them on the subject; but even among them there were father-love and marriage. Marriage among them was a purely juridical institution defining the obligation of a man in respect to the economic support he was expected to

Are Marriages Made in Heaven?

give his wife in the matter of rearing her children. A man married the woman he loved and went on loving her children and supporting them as a matter of course, completely in the dark about his biological relation to his children, but thinking that it was in the nature of women to bear children when they mature, much in the same fashion as people who know nothing about the sex-life of plants take the natural fertility of mature plants for granted.

Of this sort of father-love Bertrand Russell writes:

"The Melanesians do not know that people have fathers; yet among them fathers are at least as fond of their children as they are where they know them to be their children. A flood of light has been thrown upon the psychology of paternity by Malinowski's books on the Trobriand islanders. . . . There are in fact two entirely distinct reasons which lead a man to be interested in a child; he may be interested in the child because he believes it to be his child, or again, he may be interested in it because he knows it to be his wife's child. The second of these motives alone operates where the part of the father in generation is unknown."*

Although we know no time in the antiquity of Indo-Aryans wherein paternity was unknown to them, there are traces in ancient Sanskrit literature of patriarchal marriage having been once a juridical institution, merely defining the economic liabilities of men in the matter of supporting women and children. Leaving aside the lascivious Tantric literature, even in the holiest of our holy texts we find reference to respectable men and women who indulged in extra-matrimonial sexual relations apparently under the sanction of the moral codes of the times. In the story of

* B. Russell, *Marriage and Morals* (George Allen & Unwin Ltd.).

Women and Marriage in India

Satyakama Jabala, related in the Chandogya Upanishad, Jabala discourages the impertinent questions of her son regarding his paternity.* We are told in the Mahabharata that Swetaketu grew wrathful at the behaviour of a guest who made advances to his mother, but was rebuked by his father for being a youth without understanding as the custom was sacred to Aryans. According to the Sastras a man can have about ten kinds of sons and "a son need not necessarily have been begotten by his father nor need he have been produced by his father's wife."

All this confusion of morals is taken as indicative of times wherein marriage among Indo-Aryans was purely juridical. It seems a man had to support his wife and her children without having any right to demand fidelity from her.

This sort of marriage might have been possible in a transitional state of society from matriarchy to patriarchy. In primitive matriarchates we find women often not obliged to be faithful to their husbands. But, patriarchal traditions getting fully established in India, the insistence on wives' fidelity as a prevention of cuckoldry must have been general. It began to be considered unnatural that a man should be compelled to toil for the support of children other than his own. In due time it was enacted that every woman should

* "(1) Satyakama Jabala enquired of his mother Jabala: 'I long to abide by a tutor as a Bramacharin; of what Gotra am I?'

"(2) She said unto him: 'I know not, child, of what Gotra you are. During my youth when I got thee, I was engaged in attending on many (guests who frequented the house of my husband) and I had no opportunity of making an enquiry on the subject. I know not of what Gotra you are. Jabala is my name and Satyakama thine. Say, therefore, of thyself, Satyakama son of Jabala.'"—Translated: Rajendra Lala Mitra. Quoted from *Hindu Sacred Books*, vol. ii. Upanishad Section, p. 79.

keep to her husband lest she plant other people's children on him, and this fidelity was sanctified in matrimony. Sanctity alone, however, was not considered efficacious. As an additional precaution we find all early Hindu law-givers enjoining on men to guard their women constantly lest their levity make cuckolds of them. In course of time fidelity became a religious duty for women. It became the most cherished virtue in a wife, the very condition of her existence. The law gave unlimited powers to a man over a woman who did not fulfil this fundamental matrimonial obligation on which the whole structure of a regular patriarchal society rests.

Thus, all the injunctions of Pathivrityam imposed upon a woman at the altar have the male fear of cuckoldry as their background.

Detailed references to the marriage customs of certain matriarchal communities would prove to us the intimate connection that exists between the sanctity of matrimony and the paternal obligation of supporting children.

Ancient Egyptians were a nation of matriarchs and among them wealth was mostly owned by women. The duty of supporting aged parents and children devolved upon women and not on men. And this is what Briffault says of their marriages:

"Marriage in ancient Egypt does not appear to have been associated with any religious ceremony. It was essentially an economic transaction and from an early date was made the subject of a written contract drawn up by a law-scribe and specifying the economic condition of the association. We possess several hundreds of such contracts dating from the Ptolemaic period and at least two from the preceding centuries. In both the latter, as well as in many of the later documents the woman is the sole contracting party and imposes her conditions on the man."*

Some of the articles of the deed are are follows:

"I (the bridegroom) acknowledge the rights of wife. From this day forward, I shall never by any word oppose thy claims. I shall acknowledge thee before any one as my wife, but I have no power to say to thee 'Thou art my wife.' It is I who am the man thy husband. From the day that I became thy husband, I cannot oppose thee in whatsoever place thou mayest please to go. I cede thee (here follows a list of possessions) that are in my dwelling. I have no power to interfere in any transaction made by thee from this day. Every document made in my favour by any person is now placed among thy deeds and also is at the disposal of thy father or of any relative acting for thee. Should anyone hand over to me any moneys that are due to thee, I shall hand them over to thee without delay and without opposition."

This was the nature of matriarchal marriage in Egypt. The contracting parties had full freedom of divorce if any of the terms of the contract were broken. Sanctity was conspicuously absent, and this among a people whose sense of the sacred was such that they used to worship every living creature and sanctify every other custom.

Nor need we go as far as Egypt to illustrate our point. The Nayars, an advanced community of Hindus inhabiting the Malabar coast, offer us an example of the sanity of marriage as opposed to its sanctity. Among them women are the hereditary proprietresses of wealth and men are but managers of property.

* R. Briffault, *The Mothers* (George Allen & Unwin Ltd.).

Are Marriages Made in Heaven?

A Nayar's marriage is a simple affair. A few relatives are invited, treated to betel leaves, and it is made known to them that Sambandham (literally, auspicious connection) has begun between the man and the girl. There are no incantations, no priests, no walking round the sacred fire, no incense-burning, no vows of eternal fidelity for better or for worse, and no beating of drums. The Sambandham announced, the bridegroom is at liberty to visit the bride in her own house at convenient times. The lady never leaves the home of her mother. Nor does the man his. Marriage is reduced to a mating arrangement without any economic or domestic disturbances. No sanctity is attached to it. Divorces are unconditional without any economic liabilities on either side.

Thus, devoid of its economic complications, we find the mystic sanctity of marriage falling to pieces. We have been persuaded to believe that it is the sexual side of marriage that is sacred whereas we find it is actually the economic side that is so.

Our objection to feminine infidelity where no economic obligation to children is involved is merely sentimental, but an objection to feminine infidelity where the obligation is involved is very real. That is why in a matriarchate sexual levity among women is treated lightly, whereas an adulteress in a patriarchate is very severely dealt with, Manu going to the extent of condemning her to the life of a jackal in her next birth and recommending, in certain cases, to speed her on her journey to the four-footed kingdom by throwing her to the dogs. And if in Russia and America feminine frailty is becoming a light matter, it is because women in these countries are coming into their own economically.

Women and Marriage in India

Economic emancipation of women inevitably drives sanctity out of matrimony.

Even those pious people who cannot talk of marriage without awe would not have failed to notice that the sanctity of our matrimonial codes is inextricably connected with the sanctity of wealth. In fact, all the institutions attendant on commercial transactions are familiar features of our marriage market too. We have in our matrimonial agents the commercial salesmen who try to palm off unmarketable goods and pocket their commission. We have interminable hagglings over dowries which are controlled by the commercial laws of supply and demand. When separations and divorces take place we find legal luminaries fixing up monetary obligations which measure our feelings of love and hatred in terms of rupees, annas, and pies. There is, too, the open selling of pretty girls by poor parents to rich old Banias in the marriage market.

Sanctity is everywhere an intimate friend of Mammon. That is why the European socialist who attacks orthodox theories of political economy without any idea of blaspheming finds himself face to face with the Pope and the Archbishop of Canterbury. That is why, too, the Indian reformer who advocates the economic independence of women finds himself accused of attacking the sanctity of the home and the hearth.

*   *   *   *   *

The political and economic forces that brought about the sanctity of matrimony in ancient India were, however, driven into the background by the religious fever that attacked the medieval world. Medieval people went crazy

Are Marriages Made in Heaven?

over God and salvation without proving the existence of either. The real home of man, according to them, was heaven or hell and this life but a vagabondage. Nothing mattered on this earth if it did not have a religious significance. Hence to make terrestrial existence bearable, they sanctified every act of life into a ritual and a religious duty. Eating, drinking, fighting, killing, sleeping, sneezing, mating, spitting—in fact, every detail of life had its taboos and its charms. The medieval age was content to live in hovels and dirty towns, but built colossal temples, mosques, and cathedrals for their gods. They suffered innumerable hardships in the name of God and perpetrated unheard of cruelties to glorify His name.

The Middle Ages were essentially an epoch of blind faith. It seems incredible to us that the forefathers of the present-day hardheaded Europeans should, on the word of a mad monk, abandon their homes and proceed, women, children, and all, with hatchets and sickles to mow down Turks in Syria. But we know for a fact that they did so and that a large part of the population of medieval Europe died like locusts in Asia Minor, driven to their doom by a blind idea. The people of Arabia, too, brought about the ruin of half humanity at the call of faith.

In India the religious idea ran riot even with greater wildness. Our motherland produced thirty-three crores and three gods which, judging from the then population of India, must work up to at least three deities per head of human beings. Our kings were beggars in comparison with the priests, so that freebooters like Mohammed of Ghazni were content to rob temples and leave kings alone.

All the perversities an idle brain could invent were practised in the name of piety in medieval India. Respectable people prostituted their wives and daughters in the name of the gods. Devotees drowned themselves in sacred rivers or threw themselves in front of the cars of riding gods to find absolution from their sins. They wrote exalting poetry (the excellence of which has never since been surpassed) in praise of their gods and sang bacchanalian airs in the same breath to please the amorous propensities of goddesses. They loved all animals on religious principles and cut the throats of goats and cocks on the same principles. They practised ascetic penances and Tantric licence, both to obtain salvation. They deified their women for their Pativrityam and burnt them alive ostentatiously for the same thing.

In this irrational frenzy (from which, by the way, India has not yet liberated herself) they deified everything and sanctified every usage; and in this mystic maze we have lost the meaning of all our institutions. Almost all the laws of our ancestors have come down to us as the laws of God and not of man. And it has become a very difficult task for us to discriminate between the laws of God and those of man and render unto man what is his and leave the rest to God.

MARRIAGE AND MORALITY

Our present code of sexual morality is founded not on the sound human insticts that necessitated the institution of marriage but on the marriage ceremony itself. Rituals and forms have driven away the substance and we are worshipping the temple whence the gods have long since departed.

A couple devotedly attached to each other may live together for life and beget children, but unless they are

Are Marriages Made in Heaven?

married by a priest they are supposed to be living in sin. A man before marriage cannot have sexual relationship with a girl he loves (and who returns his love) without being immoral and sinful. But he can even violate a girl if he can, by paying a small fee, persuade a priest to repeat certain incomprehensible words in a dead language. Then his act of violence becomes moral and even pious.

Thus we have in the marriage ceremony a magic instrument which can change an act of sin into an act of piety. Belief in this imaginary power of the marriage ceremony drives many worthy people to excesses which otherwise they would not dream of indulging in. The belief that a man properly married by the Will of the Almighty is above the laws of hygiene and decency is so deep-rooted that those who question its sanity are branded as infidels.

Marriage or no marriage, moderation is the key-note of happiness in sexual life. But, unfortunately, married life as it is lived to-day makes moderation very difficult to achieve. The convention that a husband and wife should cling to each other through thick and thin, that they should love each other and enjoy each other's company as long and as often as possible, the convention, in fact, that marriage unites a man and woman into one flesh, is taken so seriously that the number of men and women who are emaciated within a short period of their married life is considerable. Monogamy, instead of serving as a brake on excesses, proves in many cases to be an incentive to them; a monogamic couple making up in frequency what they lack in variety.

The marriage ceremony is taken not only as a sanction for domestic sexual licence but also as a substitute for courting and love-making.

Women and Marriage in India

It will be found that in nature coitus is the natural climax of courting. The female being sexually passive, she has to be roused to the joys of sex experience. To stimulate desire in the female a preliminary showing-off by the male is essential and for this purpose Nature has endowed the male in all forms of higher life with abundant material for attraction. The plumage of the peacock, the mane of the lion, and the beard and noble bearing of man are all Nature's devices by the display of which the female may be attracted and "captured." No female suffers herself to be "caught" till she is sufficiently roused. Every ideal sex-act, whether in man or in beast, must be preceded by courting.

But a married man has no necessity for attracting his wife in any way, courting her before the sex-act, rousing her, or "capturing" her. The marriage ceremony has done all these things for him. No woman can refuse her favours to her husband. All that a married man need do by way of courting his wife is to order his pleasure. Even this is often dispensed with. A dutiful wife is supposed to know her husband's wishes before they are expressed.

If a man finds pleasure in such a sex-life, it is far from being a healthy pleasure. As for the woman, in her heart of hearts she detests her husband for reducing an act of supreme joy to an act of repugnance. And most of our family brawls can be traced to this undesirable element.

Perhaps the most obnoxious feature of our marriage code is child-marriage. In communities practising this form of sadism, the newly-wedded girl is always a child while the husband often happens to be a sturdy man already married more than once. And the results of such unions are the reverse of happy. Although consummation does not generally take place till the girl shows signs of maturity, there are cases wherein it does happen before puberty, with what results can better be imagined than explained. In any case, the experience of what they call "the first night" is a revelation to the girl and after the horrors of this night she can look upon her husband only as a heartless villain. It is not seldom that after this experience the girls run to homes of their parents and refuse to return to their husbands. But, according to the code, they have to be brought back and handed over once more. Nothing so iniquitous could be practised outside the limits of our marriage code; and no wonder this morality had to be sanctified to be effective.

Then there are the tales of broken pelves. Although they are by no means so numerous as to support the stories of our American critic, yet truth compels us to admit that these things do occur under the sanction of conventional morality in spite of the Sarda Act. The Sarda Act has not brought about any appreciable change in the morality of the people in British India, to say nothing of the native States where the Act does not operate. The objection brought about by the Act is, it must be remembered, legal and not moral.

All these undesirable aspects of marital morality are but offshoots of its essential vice, which is the absolute power the marriage ceremony gives a man over a woman. In certain respects this power is more despotic than that enjoyed by political tyrants. Marriage gives a man power to condemn an innocent woman to confinement in a cell he calls his home. It gives him power to disrobe a woman whenever he wants to and even against her will. It gives him power to demand work from her without remuneration. It gives a man afflicted with leprosy or any unmentionable disease power to inflict it upon a woman in the most effective way. It gives a man the right to beat a woman even without provocation. (Recently, a magistrate in South India acquitted a man charged with wife-beating on the ground that wife-beating is permitted by Hindu Law. The High Court, however, set aside his decision. If this, however, is the view of enlightened magistrates, the attitude of the populace can very well be imagined.)

All told, marriage gives a man power over the body and soul of a woman to such an extent that she is not allowed even to think of another man. Nor do the exactions of a husband end with his death. A dead husband is worse than a living one and the lot of a Hindu widow is worse than that of a wife.

Of course, the laws of the State do not confirm all these male rights over women. But in sexual morals in India the unwritten law of society is the only law recognized, and society gives a man all the above-mentioned powers and a dutiful wife is expected to submit to them. True, many men do not exercise them all. But there is a sufficient number of men who do, to make them very objectionable. Besides, they are such that, human nature being what it is, no man can be safely trusted with them.

It may be pointed out that in spite of these iniquitous codes there are many happy homes in India, where relations between husbands and wives are cordial and even exemplary. But these happy relations, I fear, must be interpreted more in the nature of the happy relations existing between certain dogs and their masters. The dog knows that it lives by permission of its master. And a woman knows, much better than a dog, that her daily bread, her happiness, and her honour depends upon the caprice of her husband and she takes infinite pains to see that she gives him no cause for complaint. Besides, some women are so gentle by nature that they are incapable of quarrelling and would get on with anybody. But as soon as a woman whose sense of independence is keener than her love of peace shows any tendency to assert her individuality, the beauty and felicity of our domestic life fall to pieces. The wife nags the husband, the husband beats his wife, the daughter-in-law rises against the mother-in-law, and the home is reduced to pandemonium. Women very often flee from such married life to the houses of their parents. But a wife being inextricably tied down to her husband for better or for worse, there is no way of permanent escape for her and she is in due time brought back to her husband only to be insulted and sent home again.

Thus, the so-called beauty of those Indian homes that claim it is the result of the low vitality of our women and not of the sanity of our moral code. And the greater the number of such happy homes in India the worse for the country.

The privileged position courtesans have been enjoying in India through the centuries to our own times throws a sidelight on our heritage of perverse moral codes. The power of the prostitute is an unerring index to the degradation of the married woman.

All medieval travellers who visited Indian cities, it will be noticed, were struck by the number of courtesans in them and the enviable position they enjoyed. Ibn Batuta speaks very highly of the Mahratha dancers of Doulatabad. He tells us how they sang and danced before mosques and temples to admiring crowds and with what freedom they reclined on couches in the shops of wealthy merchants, attended by slaves and maid-servants. European travellers like Bernier and Tavernier also speak of the ubiquitous Nauch girl who was as much in demand in the palace and the temple as in the street. Going further back, Sanskrit literature bears witness to the power of the harlot. Apart from stray references in well-known works, Damodara Gupta in his *Kuttanimatham* (Lessons of a Bawd) teaches the art of seduction to young girls entering the profession. Nor did such an accomplished writer as Kshemendra think it beneath his dignity to write his pornographic work, *Samayamatrika* (Harlot's Breviary).

Of the harlots of medieval India E. P. Mathers observes: "They were objects of sympathetic admiration, and were considered the glory and ornaments of the city. They were in evidence at all public festivities, in religious processions, at race meetings, at the cock-fighting, quail-fighting, and ram-fighting, and were the stars of each theatrical audience. Kings showered favours upon them and took counsel with them; they come down to us as the heroines of plays and romances.

"In the *Jataka* we read of them as receiving a thousand gold pieces for a night, and in the *Taranga* of Katha, one of them demands five hundred elephants for a single hour. In the latter work, too, a prostitute is so rich that she can buy an army to restore a fallen king.

"The reason for the truth which underlies these extra-vagances is not far to seek. The division, shared with so many other communities, of women into two classes—those bound and fecund for service of the hearth and race, those free and vowed to barrenness as a condition of their beauty— grew much deeper in Hind under Brahman authority and the caste system. Long before "the Lessons of a Bawd" was written, the condition and influence of the wife had become

30

negligible. She had no education and never knew an independent thought, passing, as she did, at a far too early age, from the authority of her mother to that of her mother-in-law. She shared her husband with others and had no intellectual intimacy with him; she could be cast aside at caprice and was despised if she remained childless. If she became a widow she was expected not to survive the widowing.

"From this status of the wife, the condition of the courtesan benefited, of course, very greatly. Her liberty was protected by law, and she could give or refuse herself. She had to be conquered, if only by money, and was thus the sole being still to be advantaged by the sexual rivalry of males. Part of her adornment was a really complete education and this education not only attracted but also protected.

"Thus, as the wife became more and more the slave, the courtesan became more and more the ideal, the thing for which to commit immortal follies. It was fashionable to ruin oneself for her; and the genuinely subtle, intelligent, educated male, though knowing all that was to be known about her would yet immolate himself."*

Such was the degradation of women caused by medieval moral codes. Nor are these conditions completely changed in India. There are still many men among us of a conventional turn of mind who treat their wives as domestic servants good enough to drudge and bear children, and seek the courtesan for the pleasures of sexual company. All our old-fashioned Zamindars count their social status by the number of mistresses they keep. Some of our temples still retain their Deva Dasies. In certain parts of India few religious ceremonies are complete without the attendance of public dancers.

* *Introduction to Eastern Anthology,* vol. i.

Women and Marriage in India

There are even castes of prostitutes who practise their trade as a religious duty. Many of you must have read the story, given wide publicity in the *Harijan* by Gandhiji, of a poor boy who, while applying for a scholarship to Gandhiji described himself as the son of a prostitute! The boy, it may be mentioned, was born in wedlock and his mother was a virtuous lady; but she belonged to the caste of prostitutes.

*   *   *   *   *

Marriage, according to Bacon, is an impediment to all great enterprises, whether of virtue or of mischief. The deterrent effect of conventional marriage on genius has been recognized throughout the ages and vigorous minds have often revolted against it. Jesus never married. He loved the society of women as any other man; he was accused of associating himself with sinners by his enemies and was suspected of weakness towards women by his own disciples; which shows that it was not due to any horror of sex that he remained unmarried. Sankara kept miles away from marriage, and Sidhartha, having tasted it, ran away from it as fast as his legs could carry him. The hostility of these great men towards marriage may be attributed to a streak of asceticism in them. But by no stretch of imagination can the misogamy of Voltaire and Queen Elizabeth be attributed to the same cause. Our living great men also do not take kindly to marriage. Gandhiji has confessed his disappointment in married life. There are others, less frank, who remain unmarried for "private reasons." There are still others, who having lost their wives remain widowers for the ostentatious reason that they love their dead wives too devotedly to contemplate union with other women.

Are Marriages Made in Heaven?

The misogamy of great men and women is generally attributed to their aversion to sex. Sex, it is said, is an impediment to the greater life. On a closer examination of the question it would be found that it is not *sex-life* that is an impediment to the greater life but *married* sex-life. Experience and history tell us that normal sex-life far from being a handicap to greatness is a positive aid to it. All the great men of history with negligible exceptions were non-celibates. The case of ascetics apart, what great men consciously or unconsciously have been in revolt against was not so much sex-life as the demoralizing atmosphere of conventional married life. Some of them knew it, and those among them who had the courage of their convictions flouted public opinion and lived, like Voltaire, in open sin. Others, perhaps sexually subnormal, did not find it difficult to remain celibate and let the whole question of marriage pass by. The rest married; but the married morality of Napoleon, Mohammed, Caesar, Byron, and Cleopatra was by no means conventional. Great men caught in conventional morality generally remain just above the average, like British statesmen.

The naked truth is that our matrimonial codes are such that people with a keen sense of decency or independence cannot stand them. In India the case is particularly deplorable. And unless we make our marriage an institution decent people can live in, many a great man will be compelled to live in sin or lead an unnatural life.

*   *   *   *   *

With many people morality means conjugal fidelity. But fidelity can be very demoralizing if one is faithful to evil. Moreover, current ideas of feminine fidelity are founded

33   C

not on sentiments but on property rights. What a man generally objects to in his wife is not simply acquaintance or intimacy with another man, *but acquaintance or intimacy with another man without his permission.* An African can lend his wife to whomsoever he pleases, but if the woman takes the initiative herself and goes over to another man without his permission, he has the right to kill her and sue the other man for damages. The modern young man in India, if he is liberal enough, does not mind permitting his wife to go for a walk with a friend or a relative of his, but would straight away suspect her of adultery if she went with the same person without his permission. The conventional Hindu or Muslim would allow his wife to set aside the Purdah in presence of men approved of by him, but would cut her throat if she took the liberty herself. Men have no objection to their wives undertaking long train journeys involving stoppage *en route* for nights with other men, provided they permit it, but would commit murder if their wives went out for an evening walk with the same people without permission. In the Niyoga even actual intercourse with another man fails to revolt conventional morality if the woman does it with the consent of her husband.

Thus it is the right of proprietorship over his wife, granted him by the marriage ceremony, that a man defends when he defends conventional morality. He is defending the rights of a man to till his own soil and resist poaching and encroachment. That is why we are but mildly critical of the promiscuity of the prostitute, who, after all, is nobody's property, but feel shocked at the infidelity of a married woman. A man who commits adultery with another man's wife is stealing property, and since a wife is considered a very treasured possession, the crime becomes the more appalling. Even when a wife is not considered a treasured possession but a positive nuisance, the husband would object on principle to other people becoming interested in her, exactly as a farmer objects to his neighbours encroaching upon land he neglects.

Treating woman as chattel is a habit that has come down to us from our ancestors. They treated women and children as property that could be changed hands. Harichandra, we are told, sold his wife and child into slavery to pay off his ill-contracted debts to a Brahmin. Yudhishtir, after dissipating all his possessions in a game of dice, calmly pawns his wife for the last deal; and Dussasana, after winning over his cousin's wife in gambling, proceeds to amuse himself by disrobing her in presence of all the assembled dignitaries of the .land. We might, of course, as decent human beings, resent this ribaldry of Dussanana. But he was strictly within the law of his times which permitted a man to do what he pleased with a woman he bought in the market or won by gambling. Again, Dussasana's insult to Draupadi was meant more as an insult to the Pandavas, her owners, than to herself. As you know, it was customary for medieval Muslim kings to parade the women-folk of a refractory chief naked through the streets to impress upon the public the gravity of their husband's treason. It was in this spirit that Dussasana insulted Draupadi.

Nor has modern India overcome this undesirable medieval heritage. Treating women as chattel still lingers among us in many subtle ways. It is, however, time we broke this habit. Nor is it merely a sense of fairplay that tells men to emancipate women. In their own interest men should do so.

Women and Marriage in India

Without free women there can be no free men. Enslaving women, men become slaves of slaves. Women's methods of subjugating men are more subtle than men's methods of subjugating women, but not the less effective. Even well-educated and cultured Indians very often find themselves ruled by their superstitious wives to whose vanity and low tastes they pander although to all outward appearances they are the masters of their own houses. A man cannot make a slave of his wife and escape slavery himself.

Our marriage morality can best be described as a vicious circle in which husband and wife chase each other into disastrous ruin.

THE FAMILY IN INDIA

It was Swami Vivekananda, I think, who deplored the scarcity of leadership in India. He attributed it to illiteracy. But illiteracy has never been an obstacle to genius. All our great men of action were more or less illiterate. Akbar, Shivaji, Hyder Ali, and Ranjit Singh had not much of letters to boast of. Ranjit was such an ignoramus that he used to keep the accounts of his treasury by cutting vertical and horizontal lines on his walking stick, but in military skill and administrative ability few Indians have excelled him. Nor is illiteracy a peculiarity of Indian geniuses. Charlemagne was illiterate. It is doubtful whether Jesus knew the art of writing. He has written nothing except some incomprehensible lines in sand. Mohammed was illiterate.

Those were different times, one may say. But what of the modern dictators of Europe and Iran, most of whom had very little of literary education?

Are Marriages Made in Heaven?

The real cause of India's poverty in leadership is the bad quality of the material rather than illiteracy. A really outstanding genius, when one is born, makes light of his surroundings and breaks through them, picks up letters if he wants them, and goes ahead carrying all before him. Education, while quite capable of raising the standard of a people, cannot create geniuses. You cannot make a genius of a man by hammering ideas into his head.

What India wants for leadership is better material in the form of better children; and these, judging from our present-day standards of matrimonial morals can only be born either in unconventional homes or out of wedlock.

The futility of matrimony and conventional home-life in the matter of producing geniuses is a very old one. Almost all the outstanding men and women of ancient India were born out of wedlock. Vyasa, the author of *Mahabharata*, was an illegitimate son of Satyavati and Parasara. Vidura, the great moralist, was Vyasa's son begotten on an unmarried Sudra maidservant. Karna, the most brilliant of Bharata heroes, was born of an unknown father to Kunti, and had to be exposed. The Pandavas were called Pandu's sons by courtesy, they being begotten on his wives by Niyoga. Pandu himself and his brother Dhritarashtra were also born of Niyoga. Shakuntala, the ideal heroine of Kalidasa and the mother of Bharata from whom India took her name Bharatam, was the daughter of Viswamitra, born of a casual connexion with a dancer.

There are more distinguished personages mentioned in the ancient books who were born out of wedlock. But there is no necessity for lengthening a list which is convincing enough already. In fact, we have reason to suspect that Indian family life, especially in medieval times, was calculated to reduce the vitality of the race and hasten the coming of the millennium wherein all life is to be merged into Nirwana, the tremendous nothing. But the few great men we had and we have were produced not on account of the soundness of our family life, but rather in spite of its weaknesses. And it is just as well that we examine our family life with a view to mending it, as, otherwise, it will have to be ended.

The family is a state within the State. It is in many respects a greater state than the national State inasmuch as the laws of the national State may be broken with impunity within the hallowed limits of the home. Whether greater or lesser than the State, it is the one vital institution of social life, for in it are the most intimate relations between men and women and the life of the future citizen is moulded. The education received in the home is the groundwork upon which every individual has to build in mature life.

In India State-education is received only by the favoured few and the vast majority of people are educated at home. Even the small education imparted by the State is so poor that it is unable to cancel the communal and other prejudices people learn at their mothers' knees. Hence, the new India cannot afford to leave the family entirely in the hands of ignorant, irresponsible people, for the sake of the sanctity of the home and the hearth. For a new India, ruled in a civilized fashion, we need a family instituted on scientific lines instead of on superstition as at present. But before demanding this new family, it is necessary to point out the defects of the present family, which, most people being accustomed to it and knowing nothing better, take to be normal and even ideal.

Are Marriages Made in Heaven?

The families that helplessly breed the unhappy millions of India can be roughly divided into two: (1) The Joint Family of the countryside and small town and (2) The Pigeon-hole Family of the industrial cities. I have left out the very rich who live in palaces and the very poor who breed in the streets and hovels, for obvious reasons.

(1) THE JOINT FAMILY is the indigenous family of India. It is a survival of the Moghul period into the twentieth century, with the nation on the threshold of democracy. Our domestic life is centuries behind our political life.

Although the wisdom of mere old age is being questioned everywhere in India and energetic young men lead in politics, industry, and public service, yet in our family life the oldest man is still considered to be the wisest man and his authority supreme. Modernism travels slowly in India, and in the villages and small towns it will be found that the head of the family is held in the same superstitious awe by the younger members of the family as he was centuries ago. Young men cannot sit with him or eat with him. In certain families, especially in South India, young men of the house cannot even talk to him except through the medium of the eldest son or a favoured individual. If necessity presses a young man to talk to his father this is reluctantly permitted; and I have seen young men talk to the head of the family from round the corner with their mouths covered by the palm of the hand lest they show teeth in the presence.

All this Sultanic distance and display of authority might have been quite becoming in the head of a family in a society founded on fear and tyranny. But gross tyranny in India died with the Moghuls and we do not want our children to grow up in perpetual fear of the king represented by the

39

head of the family. We want our children to grow up in that loving, sympathetic atmosphere which alone can draw the best out of them. Fear thwarts instincts and thwarted instincts lead to many melancholy results in children.

Overcrowding is a common feature of our joint families. It is not seldom that sixty to eighty men, women, and children live in one of these families and the tumult and the shouting in it is reminiscent of a village fair. As an institution of self-defence the family with a dozen young men and a hoary patriarch to lead them might have been appropriate in medieval times. But the Thugs and the Pindaries have disappeared and the young men, now that there are no dacoits from whom to defend their homesteads, take to fighting among themselves.

Economically, too, the joint family is a failure in modern India. Young men are half-educated in schools and colleges, and they think it demeaning to follow the ancestral occupation of agriculture or shop-keeping. They are all for Government service and with the present alarming rate of unemployment among the educated middle-class youths, most of them are left in the air. They form a drain on the resources of the family and of their elder brothers who are in service. And as long as they have these resources to fall back upon, the tendency of the majority of them is to become lazy and to prey upon the family income. Early marriage aggravates the evil and a young man before he finds a job often finds himself the father of two or three children. And these go to swell the burden of the family. And lastly, the fact that the energetic and successful will have to waste their earnings on the wasters, tends to serve not only as a deterrent to individual enterprise, but as a perpetual cause of strife.

Are Marriages Made in Heaven?

The ideas of sex obtaining in joint families are superstitious. All the taboos are vigorously enforced by the elders who are past the age for experiencing sexual pleasure. The sex-life of the young is a clandestine affair, a deadly sin practised under cover of night in the security of a locked room. Any familiarity between the sexes, whether it be between husband and wife, brother and sister or cousin, immediately involves the censure of the elders. The segregation of the sexes is so rigid that when opportunities arise young men and women are often driven to incest.

The miseries of the male members of the joint family are much mitigated by the freedom males have in an outdoor life. They escape the tyranny of the home in the labours of the field, the wranglings of the village Panchayat, the pleasantries of the riverside, and the gossip of the village coffee-shop. Moreover, they have the opportunity of free social intercourse with the outside world and come across many people, the educative influence of which stands them in good stead in getting on with the other members of the family. But the lot of women is different.

Women in joint families seldom move about or meet people, and, the prejudice against female education being what it is, the scope for social intercourse is extremely limited. The patriarch of the family is a liberal as compared with the mother-in-law, who is in charge of the Zenana. Her power of domestic persecution is provervial and she is by common consent the most objectionable feature of the joint family. She had been smarting under the wrongs of her own youth perpetrated on her by her elders and now that she has come into power she sets about to avenge them. But in this world it is seldom that the guilty suffer and she

41

works her pent-up venom upon her innocent daughters-in-law. If one of these girls happen to be pretty and vivacious she is marked down as a special target since, according to the moral codes of the mother-in-law, good looks and vivacity are the attributes of prostitutes. The old lady has lost her own beauty and youth but must not be supposed to be more virtuous on that account; hers are the sins of the bones and not of the flesh. Having nothing else to do in the house but nag her daughters-in-law, she sets up one girl against another and enjoys the fun. She shows marked preference to those girls who bring ornaments and sweets to her household from theirs. She shows her superiority to the mother of her daughter-in-law by insulting the innocent girl without provocation. Any absent-mindedness in the girl is used as evidence against her breeding and a reflection on her mother. If the poor girl, worn out of patience, complains to her husband, as at times happens, and if the latter so much as throws a hint to his mother, Cain is raised and the daughter-in-law denounced as a witch who enchanted her husband to rise against the mother that suckled him. And, the mother-in-law, being a comparatively free woman by virtue of her wrinkles, goes about the neighbourhood carrying tales against her daughter-in-law and canvassing public opinion in favour of herself.

When the son dies, she acquires an additional weapon with which to plague the poor widowed girl. The man's death is directly attributed to her on the principle that a Hindu woman, if she be virtuous enough, can prevent the death of her husband or even reclaim him from death like Savitri. And as no sin can be fully expiated but through suffering, the mother-in-law takes upon herself the task of

Are Marriages Made in Heaven?

persecuting the widow. All the drudgery of the house, henceforward, is the lot of the widow. Her hair is shaved off and she is shunned as an omen of evil and hounded from everywhere as a bringer of evil. Young or old, she must always be careful to make her personal appearance as repugnant to herself and to others as possible. Any attempt at looking in the mirror, putting on presentable linen, humming a tune or smiling or jesting, brings down the wrath of the mother-in-law who wants to know if the cause of the girl's pleasantry is the absence of her husband. Even when truth demands that the question should be answered emphatically in the affirmative decorum demands that she should pull a long face and retire to a corner. The widow in a joint family often wonders why the benevolent custom of Sati was abolished.

Only those who have lived in a joint family know what a pandemonium it is, especially for women.

Though it is true that ignorance and superstition contribute substantially towards this state of affairs, the main cause of the trouble is the inherent weakness of the joint family system. Where over a score of men and women in a primitive state of mental development with their full complement of children live together in a congested place and feed in the same kitchen, a peaceful, healthy atmosphere is beyond hope. Against this fundamental weakness of the joint family a theory is advanced that it is in the nature of blood-relations to love one another under all conditions. But experience and history disprove this theory. There were few kings in India who ascended their thrones except over the dead bodies of their blood-relations. The fratricidal wars of the sons of Shah Jehan all but brought about the disintegration of the

Women and Marriage in India

Moghul Empire. The Mahabharata war, too, was fought among blood-relations. Even now litigation between brothers is a common feature of our joint families and the number of families ruined by such law-suits is quite considerable. All this makes us even suspect that blood-relationship, instead of being an incentive to love, is provocative of mutual destruction, since affection among relatives is, by its very nature, imposed and not voluntary.

Be that as it may, the joint family is no place for the growth of healthy children. Children know it instinctively and hence their tendency to linger about streets and play-grounds and defer going home until goaded by hunger or the rod.

These beautiful homes of ours are, however, rapidly breaking up under the pressure of modern conditions and are giving place to the other den of middle-class vice, namely:

(2) THE PIGEON-HOLE FAMILY OF THE CITY.—This family is a recent development in Indian social life and it is generally brought about in the following manner.

An unmarried young man with a degree or a matriculation certificate and some initiative uproots himself from a joint family and drifts towards one of the big cities in search of work. Supposing that he does not turn tramp or end in suicide, he manages to find work with a poor pay. The old wolf thus kept at bay, he looks for the amenities of civilized life. He grows tired of the unwholesome food of cheap hotels. He is a stranger in the city, is lonely and yearns for companionship and the joys of social life. Then there is the ever-present urge of sex. He cannot make love to other men's wives, as all married men in the city shut their women up in their brick-box houses and will not allow the landlord

Are Marriages Made in Heaven?

to rent a house to a bachelor with seven buildings distance. There are no free women to take an interest in him, for in girlhood women are the property of their parents and in youth of their husbands. There are some old hags, it is true, who are tolerably free, but to them one cannot make love. The fear of unmentionable diseases and the want of money keep our hero out of the brothels, to which be added the dread of sin. He is born a poor man in this life and has ambitions of a head-clerkship in the next. All these considerations make him a staunch believer in marriage. Marriage solves all his problems. He acquires in his wife an honest servant to cook his food, to keep his brick-box clean, to wash his clothes, and to press his legs when he comes home tired from office. He gets delightful bed-company, too. And what is significant, he need not pay for these services. If he is lucky enough to belong to a community wherein girls are given away with dowry, he acquires some cash also.

Once he marries and achieves his "family" he becomes a respectable man, a hater of bachelors, a moralist, and a responsible individual, competent to reproduce the race. Now that he has the sanction of ancient Rishies to commit sin, he indulges in it with impunity. He loses interest in everything except his home. He suffers himself to be bullied in his office in the calm confidence that he can pass it all on to his wife. He becomes, in short, the legendary Babu of India. But what about his wife?

A woman in a pigeon-hole family lives in a sort of solitary confinement. She has very few household duties as the house is very small and almost all articles of food are brought home by the husband. Cooking is a simple affair and occupies little time. Sitting all alone in the house she becomes indolent and develops, as Manu says, a love for her bed and her seat. By way of congenial conversation, she has to hear all the long and sorry tales of office work with which her husband plagues her. Although she has not even an academic interest in them, as a dutiful wife she listens to them all with rapt attention, and she hates her husband the more because of it.

This family is a bastard form of the European family and is, like all our misguided imitations, a failure. In Europe the man has his club, his sports, and the tavern, and the woman has her marketing, her church, and even the cinema. The Babu, on the other hand, has only his home, and the wife being the home, as Viswamitra tells us, she is his club, his playground, and the tavern. And since he knows nothing better than this sort of home, he, like Tagore's chick that is mortally afraid of breaking the security of the shell, has an exaggerated idea of the comforts of home life and is terribly afraid of the home being broken up by modern conditions.

Whenever the robust European woman finds her husband too home-loving or sentimental, she manages to nag him into his club or the cricket-field. But her Indian sister is too much of a Pathivrita to do anything of the sort. She stands dutifully on the balcony from 5 p.m. onwards, watching her lord come home from office, tries to smile and look pleasant when he comes, proceeds to undress him, puts him to bed, presses his lean limbs and long head, feeds him out of her hand, and generally makes him the voluptuous imbecile he is. And there are people who extol all this as the virtue of an Indian wife and the beauty of home-life. Under these conditions it is not to be wondered that an inverse ratio is maintained between the beauty of our home-life and the quality of the race.

Are Marriages Made in Heaven?

Many of the children produced in these homes are morons, ending up in the street or on the banks of the Ganges. The more fortunate become distinguished individuals in the shape of clerks in government offices. As for leadership, you can look for it elsewhere.

*   *   *   *   *

These two kinds of family cannot produce healthy, normal children, let alone heroes and leaders. In point of fact, the joint family has many redeeming features as compared with the pigeon-hole family. For one thing, the larger member-ship of the joint family and the fights they put up one against another sharpen the intellect of those children who are not killed by it and they can fight the battle of life better than those brought up in the brick-box family. For another, the children of the joint family are kept, through neglect, for long periods out of its poisonous atmosphere, in the streets and in the playgrounds, whereas those born in the pigeon-hole families are spoiled by the cuddling of their mothers who find no other outlet for their sensuous natures. Considered as places for the birth and education of responsible citizens of an independent India, both forms are dens of unredeemed vice.

Yet, it may be argued, India has a number of leaders. True. But where do our leaders come from? From above and not from below. That is why, barring one or two exceptions, our leadership these two centuries has been so poor. All great leadership rises from below, as witness the modern dictators of Europe, all of whom rose from the street. But in India even socialist leaders have to come from the aristocracy. It will also be noticed that none of our living leaders come from a conventional Indian home but from aristocratic and well-to-do families which, through English education and by judicious selection, have combined in them the good points of the Eastern and Western family life. Such families are very rare in India and this is the cause of the poverty of Indian leadership. Again, it is not every ideal family that produces a hero. What we ought to do is to increase the number of such families so that the country may have a chance not only of throwing up an occasional genius, but also of raising the average level. And it may also be mentioned that, without overlooking the necessity of leadership in crises and periods of transition, in a democracy the average citizen is more important than the hero.

CHAPTER II

Subjection of Women in India

★

THE biblical story of the creation first of man, and then of woman as an afterthought of Jehovah (a story Hindus believe all the more readily because of its tendency to establish masculine precedence) is a myth invented by the writer of Genesis to give theological sanction to the dominance of man over woman. Science bears witness against Adam and points to the precedence of Eve.

There are certain biological data which point to a phase in the evolution of life, probably intermediary between reproduction by division and the perfection in sex of reproduction by combination, wherein females alone were capable of reproducing the species. There are many forms of life extant (brine-shrimps, ostracods, saw-flies, etc.) among which females are capable of reproducing the species without the participation of the males. These are, perhaps, survivals from a remote biological age of mothers. The insignificance and superfluity of the spermatozoa as compared with the ova, too, show the importance of the female in the matter of reproduction and support theories of primeval feminine self-sufficiency.

Be that as it may, we have sufficient anthropological evidence to prove that civilizations that to-day are patriarchal have a matriarchal ancestry. This theory of universal primitive matriarchy supplies a key to the enigma of the ascending scale of feminine freedom which we find in tracing the status of women in India backwards from the Middle Ages to prehistoric times.

UNIVERSAL PRIMITIVE MATRIARCHY*

When human society struggled into existence out of the animal world, mankind brought with itself many of the instincts of its ancestors which supplied the background for its institutions. In the jungle we find that the herd instinct is stronger in females than in males. The animal family generally consists of the mother and her young. The herds of most of the herbivora consist solely or mostly of cows. Even in herds in which males are included, the duty of watching, spying, and scouting devolves upon old females who perform their duties so scrupulously that when a herd is attacked these mothers fight to the last and die at their posts. When the hunter of big game meets a pair of African lions, he takes care to shoot the lioness first, for the male generally makes off after the fall of his mate, whereas the female would fight with revengeful fury on the fall of the male.

The female is a more tenacious defender of the cause and the herd than the male. In her is implanted more strongly the altruistic instincts of suffering for a cause, the sacrifice of self-interest for the sake of posterity. Mother-love is the

* For exhaustive evidence in support of this theory, the reader is referred to *The Mothers*, by R. Briffault (George Allen & Unwin Ltd.). I have to acknowledge my indebtedness to this excellent work from which most of the quotations under this sub-heading are taken.

fountain-head from where flow all the streams of love, sympathy, and pity.

Thus it was only natural that in the most primitive form of human society women were the guardians of the tribe and that their rights took precedence over those of men. Many of the primitive societies now extant also bear testimony to this fact; with a few exceptions we find in all of them that women dominate men in every sphere of social life. The land and cattle are considered to be the sacred possession of mothers. Man is master only of casual wealth, such as the game he hunts and the cattle and victuals he steals or loots from a neighbouring tribe. Even these, once they are brought to the hut, come under the control of women. White men who first encountered primitive communities were much intrigued to note that the man whom they took to be the master of the house could not dispose of two cowries' worth of goods without the permission of his wife or little daughter. All the property belonged to women, and marriage either brought to the household a worker in the form of the husband or was a mating arrangement without either the man or the woman ever leaving the homes of their mothers.

In Formosa, we are told, the husband after marriage goes to live in the house of the wife to toil for her. The same arrangements, with slight modifications, are noticed among the Esquimaux, the bushmen of South Africa, and many of the aborigines of East Africa, Sumatra, and Australia. Nor is this domestic arrangement so barbarous as we take it to be. The report of European missionaries who went to teach the American matriarchs the felicity of Christian domestic life throws much light on the matter.

"The domestic life of the Zunis," says Mrs. Stevenson,

51

Women and Marriage in India

"might well serve as an example to the civilized world. They do not have large families and the members are deeply attached to one another." "The house," says Dr. Kroeber of the same people, "belongs to the women born of the family. There they come into the world, pass their lives, and within their walls they die. As they grow up, their brothers leave them each to abide in the house of his wife. Each woman too has her husband or succession of husbands sharing her blankets. So generation succeeds generation, the slow stream of mothers and daughters forming a current that carried with it husbands, sons, and grandsons."

Again, "my own personal knowledge of the matriarchal community," says E. B. Taylor, "belongs to one of the most picturesque experiences of my life on a visit made in 1884 under the auspices of the American bureau of ethnology. . . . How much kindlier and milder the conditions of these people are than what we associate with the name of savages may well be judged from the idyllic record of life among them by Mr. Cushing. He describes how a Zuni girl, when she takes a fancy for a young man, conveys a present of hewebread to him as a token, and becomes affianced, how he sews clothes and moccasins for her and combs her hair out on the terrace in the sun. With the woman rests the security of the marriage ties; and it must be said in her high honour that she rarely abuses the privileges; that is, never sends her husband to the home of his fathers unless he richly deserves it."

In spite of theories of cave-man marriage, it is more likely that in the primitive world matrimonial obligations were constituted more or less along these lines. But, with the march of time, agriculture was invented and improved upon

Subjection of Women in India

and men gave up their hunting habits and took to a settled life. In other words, man became domesticated. And with this domestication of man began the degeneration of women. Primitive man, essentially of a roving temperament and ill-suited to domesticity, impatient of restraint, and assertive, set about to reduce his mother and wife to his will. He found, too, that it paid him to own women. Agriculture was mainly a feminine occupation and to own women meant better economic stability than hunting precarious game in the forest. Thus began with the invention of agriculture and the progress of social life a gradual subjugation of woman by man.

While all ancient communities had to change to patriarchates before attaining a sound standard in civilized life, to the eternal honour of Egyptians, it must be mentioned that they were the only race among the ancients who attained a high level of civilization along matriarchal lines. The rights of these ancient mothers and the judicious use they made of them fill us with admiration for Egyptian womanhood as well as for the chivalry of their men. The privileges of the fair sex among them were thus described by Herodotus:

"In this country (Egypt) the women leave to their men the management of the loom in the retirement of the house, whilst they themselves are engaged abroad in business or commerce. . . . The men carry burdens on their heads; women on their shoulders; women stand erect to make water, men stoop. . . . The men are under no obligation to support their parents if unwilling to do so, but the women are."

Another ancient authority, Diodorus Siculus, tells us that "in Egypt queens are more honoured than kings and the

Women and Marriage in India

influence of women is greater also in private life. In contracts of marriage, it is stipulated that woman shall be mistress of her husband and that he shall obey her in every particular."

The articles of their marriage contract are mentioned elsewhere and need not be repeated here. Women were so honoured and their authority was so great that there was a proverb among the ancients that "the feet of an Egyptian woman could wander wheresoever she pleases and no one can oppose her."

Egyptian women lost their freedom and their privileges by the conquest of their country by Persians and Greeks who had already subjected their women and were spreading patriarchal theories of social life among other nations.

Briffault tells us that the Jews, the most confirmed of present-day patriarchs, once were also matriarchal. Israel takes its name from Sarah. According to the Talmud, the four matriarchs, Sarah, Rachel, Leah, and Rebecca were more respected than the patriarchs Abraham and Isaac.

The story of Eve and the Apple is an acknowledgement of woman's power to decide the fate of mankind. In the curse of the serpent, humanity is referred to as the seed of Eve. The wording of the curse of Eve, too, is significant. "Unto the woman he (Jehovah) said: 'I will greatly multiply thy sorrow and thy conception. In sorrow thou shalt bring forth children and *thy desire shall be to thy husband and he shall rule over thee.'* "

Thus, the myth of Eve and the serpent presupposes a society wherein the desire of woman was not that of her husband and wherein she was not ruled over by her husband.

Countries and continents throughout the ancient world were called after women, proof enough that land, mother of

54

Subjection of Women in India

all wealth, was identified with or owned by women. Europe was called after Europa. Asia after the wife of Prometheus, and Lybia after a lady of that name. We call the land of our birth Mathrubhoomi (motherland) and not Pithrubhoomi. Woman was the earth, the stable and steady, as the ancients conceived her and man, the roving sun, the changing sky, and the fleeting winds.

Briffault, by compelling evidence, to quote which would be beyond the scope of this book, shows that the Teutons, the Celts, the Latins, and the Yellow races all had matriarchal ancestors. Nor have we any reason to believe that Indo-Aryans are an exception to this general rule. All evidence points in fact to the contrary.

MATRIARCHY IN INDIA

As already pointed out in the first chapter, there are unmistakable traces in the Vedas and the Puranas that Vedic Indians had a matriarchal ancestry. The primordial Sakti of the Indo-Aryans, "from whom everything proceeds and who pervades everything and is conterminous with the Supreme Being himself, who is without beginning or end and is vaster than the universe" is, unlike the Hebrew Jehovah and the Muslim Allah, a female principle.

Most of the tribes and individuals mentioned in the Vedas take their names from their mothers and not from their fathers. Commenting on this as well as on the sexual freedom enjoyed by women in ancient India, Abinas Chandra Das remarks: "It is possible that at a certain stage in early Aryan society promiscuity may have been in vogue and society in that stage was, according to Dr. Shama Shastri, 'maternal or matriarchal rather than paternal or patriarchal. Words such as Daityas, sons of Diti, Vainateyas, sons of Vinata, Kadraveyas, sons of Kadru, Anjaneya, son of Anjana, Jabala, son of Jabala, and Jaratkara, son of Jaratkaru are taken as indicative of the uncertainty of the real begetter and the unsettled conditions of society which rendered promiscuity among women a necessary evil.' " (Rig Vedic Culture.)

This comment, however, cannot be accepted without qualification. The fact that in a particular community people are called by their mothers' names need not necessarily be indicative of the uncertainty of the real begetter. In most of the matriarchal communities fatherhood is known and recognized but descent is counted through the mother. Therefore, the fact of a man being known by his mother's name should be taken as indicative of the dominance of women in that society rather than the uncertainty of his father.

Whether ancient Indo-Aryans were promiscuous or not depends upon what meaning we attach to the word promiscuity. If promiscuity is taken to mean absence of marriage we must definitely say that Indo-Aryans were not promiscuous. We know of no time in their antiquity wherein they lived without marriage. But if we take promiscuity to mean extra-matrimonial sexual freedom, we have to say that Indo-Aryans were more or less a promiscuous race. This promiscuity, however, should not be imputed to any inherent vice in the matriarchal social structure, as is the rule with most writers. We must rather put it down to the primitive state of morality that obtained in those times. In thoroughly evolved matriarchates we find sexual relationship to be as sound as in any patriarchal society, whereas we find

Subjection of Women in India

a considerable laxity of morals in a primitive society even when it is patriarchal. In a matriarchate, as developed as the Egyptian, sex relationship could be not only as moral and decent as in any patriarchate, but in many respects even a definite improvement. The economic preference sanctioned by law to women weighed against many disabilities women as a sex have in acquiring wealth and it created a more balanced society than a patriarchal one.

Nor need we confine ourselves to *a priori* arguments or dig up hieroglyphics to discover how a matriarchal community works. We have in our midst a living example of a highly evolved matriarchate in the Nayars of Malabar. An insight into their domestic and social life would dispel much of the misunderstanding about matriarchy and provide proofs as well to support the belief in pre-Vedic matriarchy, for there is reason to believe that the Nayars are Aryans whose forefathers migrated from the north in prehistoric times.

The Nayars are an enigma to the ethnologist. Surrounded by Dravidians and emigrant Brahmins, they are an island community of matriarchs with very little in common with either of these neighbours. Their features, their bearing, their complexion, their legends, and their traditions all point to an Aryan origin, although their social structure is entirely different from that of the Indo-Aryans of the later days. The wide social and cultural gulf that divides the Nayar from the Pulayan, the Malayan and the Ulladan rules him out of any aboriginal origin. Under these circumstances may one not suggest that one of those groups of adventurous, sea-faring Indo-Aryans who set up colonies in Java and other islands of the Indian Ocean wandered into the coast of

Women and Marriage in India

Malabar and, protected by the sea and the Ghats, preserved the ancient social structure of Aryan society which everywhere else underwent radical changes?

The history of Malabar is intimately connected with the warrior-priest Parasurama. There is a legend among the people that he reclaimed the strip of land from Goa to Comorin from the sea-god Varuna and made a present of it to his Brahmin followers. Shorn of its mythical pretensions, the legend means that Parasurama conquered Malabar in his campaigns against Kshatriyas and distributed the land among his Brahmin followers. That he divided the land among the Brahmins requires no proofs, for even to-day all land in Malabar is owned by Nambudiri Brahmins. The Nayars themselves have a tradition that they were Kshatriyas once, that they were defeated by Parasurama and that he suffered them to live in dependence on the Brahmins on abandoning caste. Parasurama was on oath to kill all Kshatriyas and he decasted the Nayars and made them Sudras. The Nayars, though nominally Sudras, now perform all the duties of the military classes, and the Nambudiri Brahmins, in spite of the discouragement of Manu, often take to wife Nayar women without in any way endangering their social status. These marriages are of course performed according to Nayar usages and the sacramental Brahmin marriage between a Nayar and a Nambudiri is forbidden.

The Nayars are a highly cultured people and the upper classes among them are landed aristocrats. They are chivalrous and brave to a fault and the Portugese and the Dutch, who had occasion to fight for and against them, have unanimously testified to their courage and loyalty. They are the only Indians who withstood the onslaught of Tippu and beat him

Subjection of Women in India

in the open field. Travancore and Cochin are Nayar states and the Maharajahs are matriarchs and not patriarchs.

Among the Nayars, women are the mistresses of their homes. When a girl marries, she does not leave her home but the husband pays her visits in her own house. Descent and inheritance are counted through the mother and a father has no right over his child. The child is known by its mother's name and surname, which does not mean, however, that its paternity is unknown. Guardianship of children rests with the mother and the maternal uncle.

The role of men in the community is not one of idleness and abject dependence as is the case of women in patriarchates. What we consider essentially masculine work remains with men. They are the labourers, the fighters, and the administrators. The rights of mothers are identified with supreme sway in the home, economic security and superiority in deciding the ties of blood. The rulership of Travancore, for example, devolves upon a man in preference to a woman, but the Maharajah's son is not the heir-apparent but his sister's son. The prince's mother must be a princess, no matter who his father.

Divorces, among Nayars, are free and unconditional. A man can sever connexion with his wife by intimating to her his intention of doing so or even by simply ceasing his visits. The woman likewise can effect a divorce by asking her brother or uncle to let her husband know that he is no more wanted. And since the children belong to the mother and her family, a divorced father is not missed even by his own children.

In spite of the ease of divorces, it is observed that it is resorted to only rarely, and that the vast majority of respectable Nayar ladies remain faithful to their husbands even in trying circumstances. The provision of unconditional divorce serves, too, as a check on any tendency of husbands and wives to maltreat each other. The fact that the couples live in different families and meet only once or twice in a week also enhances the love between husbands and wives.

Penalties attaching to illegitimacy and unfaithfulness are slight as compared with patriarchal standards. But these standards are now recognized to be unnecessarily cruel. The Nayar punishment of mild social censure is a more sane one.

It is true that poor Nayar women, pressed by economic necessity, form transient connexions, especially with the Tamil Brahmins who come to Malabar for trading purposes. But this should be regarded as a form of prostitution and "the oldest profession," it must be remembered, is no exclusive Nayar vice. This form of prostitution is, in fact, preferable to our city brothels. Moreover, hemmed in on every side by powerful patriarchates of Brahmins, who take advantage of the matriarchal structure of Nayar society, a certain degree of abuse among the Nayars is inevitable, especially among the lower classes.

The above is a general description of the peculiar characteristics of Nayar society, which we have reason to believe, as already mentioned, is an Aryan matriarchate. Pre-Vedic society must have been developing along these lines when its progress was checked and turned into a patriarchal channel. Vedic literature, no doubt, is generally indicative of the dominance of men over women. But Vedic women were by no means the chattels and playthings of men as were women in the medieval period. They had retained much of their old independence and men dared not treat them lightly. Their

Subjection of Women in India

lot should be considered as enviable in comparison to that of women of later times.

Rig Vedic hymns show that in those days women took part with men in every activity of life whether it was the toil of the field or the pleasures of a festival. They even went out with men to fight marauding tribes and cattle-lifters. If men could sing the praises of gods and goddesses, there were lady-Rishies, too, who could compose hymns. Ghosha, Lopamudra, Mamata, Apala, Saci, Indrani, and Viswavara were some of these lady-Rishies. "The last-named lady not only composed verses in praise of Agni or Fire, but even performed the function of a Rtvij or priest at a sacrifice, which privilege was denied to women in a later age by a jealous and illiberal priesthood."

In one of the hymns* to the Maruts (the storm gods), these are mentioned as lovers courting Vak who is likened to a courtly, eloquent woman. According to Max Muller, the hymn "throws a curious light on the social character of Vedic times, as it presupposes two classes of wives—not necessarily simultaneous, however—a housewife, who stays at home and is not much seen, and a wife who appears in public and takes part in the society and conversation of the Sabha, the assembly room, and the Vedathas, the meetings."

* 3. Thus clings to the Maruts one who moves in secret like a man's wife (the lightning), and who is like a spear carried behind, well-grasped, resplendent, gold-adorned; there is also with them Vak (the voice of thunder) like unto a courtly eloquent woman.

6. As soon as the poet with the libations, O Maruts, had sung the song at the sacrifice, pouring out Soma, the youthful men (the Maruts) placed the young maid in the chariot as their companion for victory, mighty in assemblies. (*Sacred Books of the East*, edited by Max Muller, vol. xxxii. *Hymn to the Maruts*, i. 167.)

Women and Marriage in India

The existence of women who took part in the deliberations of assemblies and whose wisdom was mighty must be traced to matriarchal times, wherein women dominated the political life of the community. Although the dominance of women in assemblies and councils is foreign to patriarchal traditions, it is noticed that in almost all primitive matriarchates the voice of women is predominant in councils. Men are, no doubt, the actual combatants, but the war-councils and cabinets are found dominated by women.

The marriage customs of Vedic Aryans bear further testimony to the freedom enjoyed by women. Child-marriages were unknown. Only grown girls were eligible for marriage and they generally made their choice from a number of suitors. There were fairs and festivals in which men and women attended and young people had many opportunities of making contact with each other.

The wedding ceremony itself throws much light on the rights of the Vedic bride. Prior to the ceremony the father of the bride tells the bridegroom: "In the attainment of Dharma, Artha, and Kama, she is not to be transgressed." The bridegroom responds: "Transgress her I will not."

In the nuptial night it is the bride who takes the initiative in the matter of sexual intercourse.

The bride who enters the home of her husband is hailed as follows:

As vigorous as the Sindhu himself, Imperial Lord of Streams,
So be Imperial Queen when thou hast come within thy husband's home,
Over thy husband's father and his brothers be Imperial Queen,
Over thy husband's sister and his mother bear supreme control.

Again,

Subjection of Women in India

Bliss-bringer, furthering thy household's welfare, dear, glad-
dening thy husband and his father, enter this home, mild to
thy husband's mother.

Be pleasant to thy husband's sire, sweet to thy household and
thy lord;

To all this clan be gentle, and favour these men's prosperity.

Nor are there any traces in the Vedas of the cult of husband worship which has become the bane of later Hindu society. Vedic widows had no obligation to remain single and there were usages, as among the Hebrews, according to which a widow could claim conjugal rights with her husband's brother. She had freedom of re-marriage, and in the Atharva Veda there is a mention of the status of the second husband in the next world. Even a plurality of husbands was not considered disreputable as in the most sacred of the Rig Vedic hymns we find Rodasi attended by numerous husbands in the form of the Maruts. The twin Aswins had only one wife among them.

Nor was marriage always considered a sacrament. "We find in the Rig Veda," to quote Mr. Das again, "an instance of a marriage by contract which goes to show that such a marriage was of a temporary nature terminable on the viola-tion of the terms of contract on which it was based. The story of Urvasi and Puruvara in the Rig Veda* shows that their marriage was based on contract and that Urvasi left her husband because he had failed to perform his part of the contract and keep his promise."

All told, although Vedic women had lost most of the privileges enjoyed by their mothers in the political life of the community, they had still a considerable degree of freedom

* x. 95.

in social and domestic affairs. A slow prejudice, however, was gaining ground even against this small freedom of women. An increasing insistence on the fidelity of women was demanded and it was ensured by making them abjectly dependent on men. While women's freedom was thus curtailed, that of men was enhanced. Their range of selection and variety became wider. Polyandry was prohibited but polygyny flourished. Courtesans also came into the scene. Those men who were not content with a plurality of wives and longed for the excitement of extra-matrimonial adventures could buy feminine charms in the bazaar.

Now Vedic women could not tolerate this sort of thing. They had no traditions of slavery to man as later women had, and no husband worship as a religious duty. If they had a tradition at all, it pointed to times when women were free and men chivalrous. They had a keener sense of their wrongs than women of our days and revolt surged in their bosoms. The result was as might be expected. They indulged in clandestine love, and paramours were entertained in their husband's houses. There were tales of illegitimate children, abortion, and the exposure of babes who could not be accounted for. The old freedom and frankness of women were gone for ever and in their place began to appear hard-heartedness, subterfuge, and honeyed words coming from hearts of granite.

Some energetic women even resorted to direct action. Pradweshi, wife of the blind Rishi Dirghatamas, we are told, threw her husband into the Ganges for proposing to legislate that a woman should have only one husband in her lifetime. But Dirghatamas saved himself by clinging to a raft and lived long enough to put his proposals into practice.

Subjection of Women in India

While all references to women in the earlier Vedic hymns speak highly of them, one or two later hymns and most of the Brahmanas evince tendencies that led up to the code of Manu. In one of the hymns it is said that "woman's love is fickle and her mind ungovernable." Elsewhere, her heart is likened to that of a hyena. According to Satapatha Brahmana, "women are given to vain things" and "it is to him who sings and dances that they most readily take a fancy." In the same Brahmana, barren women are said to be possessed by the demon Nirriti.

In the Taitereya Brahmana women are referred to as always asking some gift as the price of their society. The general tone of the Brahmanas suggests that women were considered as a necessary evil. Fathers fervently prayed for sons. As for daughters, the gods were requested to give them elsewhere. The Aitereya Brahmana cries that "daughters are a cause of misery."

All this should be taken as proof that our mothers did not take kindly to their loss of freedom but gave their husbands and fathers an anxious time.

THE YOKE

The Rishies felt that the time for reforms had come. But, instead of making the laws more liberal as the times suggested, they set out to make the laws of matrimony more rigid in their exactions on wives. Now that the fidelity a woman feels spontaneously for the husband of her choice had gone, men decided to reclaim it with the aid of the policeman. A series of laws were enacted to bring woman under the will of man.

Women and Marriage in India

Most of these laws have come down to us in the code of Manu.

The code of Manu is the most sacred of Hindu Law books. To this day all orthodox Hindu institutions draw inspiration from it. Manu's authority is considered infallible and all minor law-givers conform to it. Manu, as he stands in the code, is a mythical figure, the progenitor of mankind. From certain passages in the Vedas it is even contended that Manu is not a proper noun but an abstract noun denoting the activities of Manas, the mind. It would be saner to regard him as the originator of law among Indo-Aryans. His ordinances, however, were interpolated by later law-givers, who took advantage of his authority and legislated in his name. The code of Manu that has come down to us is the effort of a number of law-givers, living at different intervals of the ancient and medieval period, and the code has a range of many centuries. For purposes of convenience, however, we will treat the code as the work of a single law-giver and refer to Manu as its author.

With negligible exceptions here and there, the whole code breathes a spirit of contempt and hostility to women. Their rights (especially those of married women) are identified with those of Sudras, slaves, and children.

To begin with, Manu ordained that a woman should never be allowed to be free. In her childhood she is to be dependent on her father, in youth on her husband, and in old age on her son; "a woman is never fit for independence"*

Manu recognizes eight forms of marriage. The most commendable forms of these are four in which the girls are not consulted, but given away by their parents as gifts to

* ix. 3.

66

Subjection of Women in India

Brahmins of varying degrees of learnedness. The Gandharava form, which is the consummation of mutual love, is branded as lust and is denounced as unworthy. Children born of it are said to be "cruel, and speakers of untruth, who hate the Vedas and the Sacred law."*

The Swayamvara form, in which a girl selects from a number of suitors, is conspicuous in Manu's code by its absence.

Vedic marriage was a sacrament to unite husband and wife into one being. But according to Manu there is no union; the wife is simply lost in the husband. "Whatever the qualities of the man with whom a woman is united according to law," says Manu, "such qualities even she assumes, like a river united with the ocean.

"Akshamala, a woman of the lowest birth being united to Vasishta, and Sarangi, being united to Mandapala, became worthy of honour.

"These and other females of low birth have attained eminence in this world by the respective good qualities of their husbands."†

Wife-beating is permitted by Manu. According to Kautilya, another ancient authority, "women of a refractory nature shall be taught manners by using such general expressions as 'Thou half naked; thou fully naked; thou cripple; thou fatherless; thou motherless.' Or three beats either with a bamboo bark or with a rope or with the palm of the hand may be given on her hips."‡

That woman is owned property is the predominant note of Manu's code. Women have no choice in marriage and are

* Manu iii. 46.   † Manu, ix. 22, 23, and 24.
‡ *Artha Shashtra*, translated: R. Shama Shastri, p. 197.

always given away in marriage. Widow marriage is not permitted because the girl has once already been given away and "no gift of the same thing can be made twice over." Men are not to commit adultery because "men who sow their seed in the soil of others benefit the owner of the woman,"* just as "if one man's bull were to beget a hundred calves on another man's cows they would belong to the owner of the cows; in vain would the bull have spent his strength."†

Of the nature of woman Manu speaks as follows:

"Women do not care for beauty, nor is their attention fixed on age; thinking it is enough that he is a man they give themselves to the handsome and to the ugly.

"Through their passion for men, through their mutable temper, through their natural heartlessness, they become disloyal towards their husbands, however carefully they may be guarded in this world.

"Knowing their disposition, which the Lord of creatures laid in them at the creation to be such, every man should most strenuously exert himself to guard them.

"When creating them Manu allotted to women a love of their bed, of their seat and of ornament, impure desires, wrath, dishonesty, malice and bad conduct.

"For women no sacramental rite is performed with sacred texts, thus the law is settled; women (who are) destitute of strength and destitute of the knowledge of Vedic texts, are as impure as falsehood, that is the fixed rule."‡

Even pure women should not be accepted as witnesses because "the understanding of females is apt to waver."§ Swearing an oath falsely even in trifling matters is con-

* ix. 51.   † ix. 50.   ‡ ix. 14 to 18.   § viii. 77.

Subjection of Women in India

sidered by Manu as a heinous crime and the man who swears
falsely is pronounced as lost in this world and the next.
However, we are told, that no serious crime is committed
by swearing falsely to women.*

Then there is the strange passage which tells us that "at
a ferry an empty cart shall be made to pay one pana, a man's
load half a pana, *and an animal and a woman* one quarter of
a pana, an unloaded man one-half of a quarter."†

In the face of this overwhelming condemnation of women,
the few stray references in which it was asked that women
be protected and well cared for, and the oft-quoted passage
in which Manu tells all men to honour their women for the
sake of their own prosperity, should be taken in the light of
a mature sage's advice to a farmer to look after his cattle
well for his own prosperity. In the whole code the mental
and intellectual qualities of woman are treated with supreme
contempt and in the selection of a wife only her physical
appearance is taken into account. Against a man's eligibility
for marriage, which is purely intellectual, a marriageable
girl should be "free from bodily defects, should have an
agreeable name, should be of graceful gait like a Swan
or an elephant, should have a moderate quantity of
hair on the body and on the head, small teeth and soft
limbs."‡

A man is not to marry "a maiden with reddish hair, nor
one who has a redundant member, not one who is sickly,
nor one either with no hair (on the body) or too much, nor
one who is garrulous or has red eyes."§

An Aryan, according to Manu, cannot eat with his wife.
"Nor look at her eating, or sneezing or yawning or sitting

* viii. 112. † viii. 404. ‡ iii. 10. § iii. 8.

69

at her ease." It seems these things disturbed the aesthetic sensibilities of twice-born men.

The days of lady Rishies, too, were gone for good. Women as a sex, were debarred from the recital of the Vedas, many hymns of which were composed by their mothers. "For a woman to recite the Vedas," we are told, "is a confusion in the realm." They were all excluded from priestly offices and they were beginning to be depised as unseemly or impure creatures before the gods. Priests saw to it, however, that things did not go so far as to exclude the Devadasies from the temple.

All told, the lot of medieval women was very wretched. They were seldom treated as decent human beings with ordinary emotions and aspirations. Woman was more or less the soil for bearing sons and even as soil the medievals overlooked its important function and believed in the self-sufficiency of the seed. As such, a woman's feelings were never consulted in the matter of her mission in life, motherhood. All that a woman was supposed to have was an unwavering fidelity to a man, very often a person not even deserving her pity, who was forced upon her by a society with perverse values of life.

The warrior castes, in spite of Manu, kept up some show of chivalry. But hemmed on every side by an exacting and watchful priesthood, their women, too, had very little of real freedom. Love's freedom of selection, in the sense we understand it to-day, never existed among them. Draupadi's marriage ceremony, which for some unknown reason is highly extolled, was merely the remnant of a custom wherein the most desirable women fell to the lot of the man with the longest sword. There is a general belief that the strongest

Subjection of Women in India

warrior makes the most lovable husband. But history tells a different tale. Wives of many a great warrior bestowed their favours on chamberlains and pages. Love's selection is irrational but profound and mature love can arise only out of mutual understanding of two people, and for this social intercourse between the sexes is necessary. Medieval society was the inveterate enemy of this right of love and the much-talked-of medieval chivalry was but an obsession of imaginary love based on hearsay, or, at best, on a glimpse of an eyebrow inadequately seen through the meshes of a veil.

The Swayamvara of Damayanthi is another story which is made too much of. While, of course, the Swayamvara is a much more liberal institution than any among the medievals, we must note that the love of Nala and Damayanthi was based upon mere talk. The poet sees through its absurdity and throws in an accident by means of which Nala was enabled to visit his love in disguise and converse with her before marriage.

Again, in the Swayamvara of Samyogita, her plans were frustrated by her father deliberately refusing to invite to the Swayamvara the man she loved.

All these instances force us to believe that the Swayamvara, which in Vedic times practised what it preached, in later times degenerated into a pompous superstition in the robes of royalty.

Nor were marriages by capture rare. It was legitimate for Kshatriyas and was indulged in even by men of unimpeachable character. Bhishma, the celibate, the wisest of Bharata moralists, captured Ambika and Ambalika from their father's house and took them to his palace for marrying them to his half-brother. Arjuna, the Pandava hero, abducted

Women and Marriage in India

Subhadra on her way to the bathing Ghat. In more recent times, the Rajput hero, Prithwiraj, who fought Mohammad Ghori, captured Samyogita from the Swayamvara Mandap and it led to an internecine war among the Rajputs.

Against all these marriage superstitions of medieval India one hears the warning of Kalidasa. With his classic love of proportion he perceived the iniquity of the whole matrimonial conventions of his times and in his immortal *Shakuntala* made Gandharva the most sublime form of marriage. In the teeth of Manu he showed that when two mature humans of the opposite sex longed to unite themselves in love for the enhancement of their own happiness and the perpetuation of life, no beating of drums, no walking round the sacred fire, and no incantations were necessary to sanctify it. He took the obscure story from the Bharata, gave it an immortal dignity and beauty and placed it before India which stood in urgent need of it. But, unfortunately, Kalidasa did not grow a long beard, and look wise. He did not smear his body with ashes and did not pretend to be in the confidence of the Almighty. He came, like the Son of Man, eating and drinking and India, seldom impressed except by contrived singularity, ignored him and followed the lead of stern perverted philosophers, who led her right down to the gates of hell.

While the primary cause of the fall of woman was man's love of power over woman, the religious idea, too, played a powerful part in deciding the destiny of Indian women. It will be interesting to trace the development of this idea which culminated in the mad fury of medieval asceticism and its manifold offshoots from which India has not yet liberated herself.

Subjection of Women in India

In Rig Vedic times we find Indo-Aryans a semi-pastoral race who had just learnt the art of agriculture. They had not yet settled down permanently and "the wants and occupations of a Vagrant life prevented them from falling into a great many superstitions which are the offspring of idleness." They were surrounded by hostile tribes and cattle-lifters against whom they had to put up a continuous fight. They had no use for lean and hungry philosophers who could wield neither sword nor club and they prayed for sturdy sons to ride fleet horses and confound the marauding Dasyus. Their gods, too, were made of the same metal. Rig Vedic Aryans did not delight in abstract principles thinner than air, but offered libations of Soma to Indra, the terrible wielder of the thunderbolt who fought and scattered the enemies of Aryans.

"The Vedic Aryans," says Sir Radha Krishnan, "entered India in the pride of strength and the joy of conquest. They loved life in its fullness. They, therefore, showed no great interest in the future of the soul. Life to them was bright and joyous, free from all the vexations of a fretful spirit. They were not enamoured of death. They wished for themselves and their posterity a life of hundred autumns. They had no special theories about life after death though some vague conceptions about heaven and hell could not be helped about reflective minds. Rebirth is still at a distance."*

Their heaven was a place "where wishes and desires are, where the region of the sun is, where food and delights are found." Rivers of Soma flowed through Vedic Paradise. For deities they were content with Indra, Varuna, and their

* Sir Radha Krishnan: *Indian Philosophy*.

relatives. They loved the pleasures of sex, but did not go out of their way to pervert them, and to indulge in the ecstacy of imaginary love. Vedic Aryans loved the hunt, a good fight, a bowl of Soma, and a game of dice.

But this simplicity of the Aryans did not last for long. Gradually they gained ascendency over their neighbours, agriculture was improved and settlements became more or less permanent. Towns and villages became policed and it was no longer necessary for all to be soldiers. Life and property thus becoming secure, the foundations of art, literature, and science were laid.

Either from the conquered races or from Persians, Babylonians, and other neighbours, or through their own innate love of speculation given free rein with the new-found security of life, Indo-Aryans began to ask questions about the First Cause and the Hereafter. They settled down to solve the riddle of life. Minor deities like Indra and Varuna did not satisfy the intellectually virile. Scientific knowledge also advanced and exploded many an accepted theory about phenomena. India entered an era of intense questioning, which, had it been conducted by well-balanced minds, would have led the country to the leadership of all nations. But, judging from results, this era proved to be the most unfortunate in India's history. Brooding and philosophic speculation became an obsession and life was reduced to a principle. Personality and individuality disappeared and dead laws reigned supreme.

As often happens in all speculative studies, the greater the number of Rishies who took to the study of philosophy the greater became the divergence of opinion. And all the philosophers developed quarrelling propensities. The number

Subjection of Women in India

of those who posed themselves as philosophers was also considerable. In fact, every Aryan who could write Sanskrit began to interpret the Vedas and no two of them could agree on any point. All, however, swore by the authority of the Vedas. Of this Vedic authority Sir Radha Krishnan says:

"The interpretation of the Vedic texts depended on the philosophical predilection of the authors. They did not wish it to be thought that they were enunciating something completely new. While this may involve a certain amount of want of frankness with themselves it helped the spread of what they regarded as truth. Critics and commentators of different schools claimed for their views the sanction of the Vedas and exercised their ingenuity in forcing that sanction when it was not spontaneously yielded."*

In other words, the philosophers enunciated their own doctrines and perverted the text to suit their convenience.

The aftermath of every religious upheaval, it would be found, has always been bloodshed and strife. While every religious teacher and philosopher was of course driven by the noble idea of propounding truth to the satisfaction of all and bringing all humanity into one unifying whole, what most, in fact, he succeeded in doing was to create a new faction of dissenters who quarrelled with all the existing factions. Buddha propounded his doctrine of the Aryan Path for the edification of mankind and created a religion which was driven out of India after almost ruining the country. Each of the six systems of Indian philosophy, with their numerous offshoots, claimed to have explained the Vedas in the only infallible way and each added one more sect to wrangle with

* *Indian Philosophy.*

Women and Marriage in India

the old. Jesus and Mohammed sought to unite all humanity under one Father, each of course in his own way, but succeeded only in creating two schools of theology the followers of which well-nigh annihilated Europe and Asia Minor. Guru Nanik, while sincerely attempting to unite Hindus and Muslims into a harmonious whole, brought forth a third dissenting faction, the Sikhs. Akbar, too, had ideas of creating a new religion for India in which all Indians were to be brothers and sisters, but mercifully he died before his ideas matured and thus saved India the humiliation of yet another religious sect.

Making every allowance for the good points in dogmas and creeds and the need of conflicts for progress, it cannot be denied that the medievals carried faith too far. Medieval Hindu history is a sad tale of the extremes to which religious beliefs can drive a people.

Some of the honest Indian philosophers who went in search of Absolute Truth and could not find it frankly admitted defeat and declared that the search is without end. The more vain, however, could not bring themselves or others to believe that they were incapable of comprehending the Incomprehensible. Such an admission wounded their intellectual vanity. Moreover, many had developed into monomaniacs in the search and they began to see visions.

Nor did the philosophers find any difficulty in deluding themselves and convincing their followers that the Vedic Paradise, "where wishes and desires are, where food and delights are found," meant a state of Nirvanic annihilation. The mention of sunrise and sunset in the Vedas were interpreted as the doctrine of rebirth according to which souls of dead men and women are reborn as dogs, mice, and mosquitoes. Ways of salvation, too, were many; some recommended works as a means, others intellectual knowledge, some ascetic penances, and others the debaucheries of Saktipuja. Some recommended devotion while others insisted upon self-realization. And all had the courage of their convictions and were ever ready to argue. The seriousness with which they engaged in polemics can be imagined from their code of honour which demanded that the defeated combatant should burn himself to death in slow fire.

Laymen who were curious to know what all this learned warfare meant were told that the great Rishies were discussing the different aspects of the Eternal Principle. Any honest man who expressed doubts and could not reconcile the "is" with the "is not" was denounced as a fool and his folly put down to Avidya (ignorance). And as all fools are afraid of betraying themselves they affected great wisdom and pretended that they knew everything.

Perversion of texts and wildness of speculation became so intolerable that sane philosophers like the Charvakas rejected the authority of the texts and the sanity of inference and maintained that perception was the only reliable guide to knowledge. Their hostility to the Vedas and to the propounders of doctrines based on them is found to be very marked. "The impostors who call themselves as Vedic Pandits," they wrote, "are mutually destructive, as the authority of the Jnana Kanda is overthrown by those who maintain that of Karma Kanda, while those who maintain the authority of the Jnana Kanda reject that of the Karma Kanda; and lastly the three Vedas themselves are only the incoherent rhapsodies of knaves and to this effect runs the popular saying:

Women and Marriage in India

'The Agnohotra, the three Vedas, the ascetics three staves and smearing oneself with ashes,

'Brihaspathi says, these are but means of livelihood for those who have no manliness nor sense.'

"Hence it follows that there is no other hell than mundane pain caused by purely mundane causes like thorns, etc.; the only supreme is the earthly monarch whose existence is proved by all the world's eyesight; and the only liberation is the dissolution of the body." *

All these conflicting theories, vigorously supported by sects, led inevitably to the astounding doctrine (which many Indians even now defend) that all forms of thought, all customs, all usages, and all superstitions were good enough for those who practised them and should be left alone. The result of this doctrine was the negation of all progress and the universal encouragement of vice and superstition. People were glad to be left alone in their blissful ignorance. It must be clearly understood that while an understanding toleration of the weaknesses of others and a sincere attempt to enlighten them to a consciousness of their failings is a nobler attitude than that of fanatical intolerance, fanaticism itself has many redeeming features as compared with a philosophy of callousness under the exalted name of universal toleration.

From this spiritual anarchy India emerged convinced of one thing: that life was evil. Thoughtful men despised life and all the joys thereof. If they lived they fulfilled the mission of life by mortifying the flesh. Extremists of this philosophy twisted their limbs, remained in uncomfortable postures for months on end without moving, hung themselves head down-

* *Sarva darsana Sangraha of Madhava Acharya*, translated: E. B. Cowell and A. E. Gough, p. 4.

Subjection of Women in India

wards from trees, slept on beds of spikes, fasted themselves unto death, walked without rest till they dropped down dead, distorted their organs, and went about unwashed and verminous, all to overcome the illusion of life through Yogic austerities.

Furthermore, woman as the more important agent in the process of reproduction was looked upon as an evil and a dangerous temptation. In woman this age saw but a "wayward animal existing solely for the propagation of the species, an end which perpetuated the woes of the world." All the sages of medieval ages were agreed that woman stood between a man and his salvation.

The spiritual and moral values of celibacy and continence were extolled to the skies. Extravagant nonsense began to be talked about the unlimited physical strength that could be obtained through Brahmacharya. The colossal strength of Hanuman was attributed to his Nitya Brahmacharya. The divine strength of his married master, however, was passed over in silence. All the achievements of married supermen like Krishna, Bhima, and Arjuna were forgotten in the praise of Bhishma the celibate. Those who sought strength of spirit tried to exclude woman from their very thoughts. But the more the ascetic shirked life, the greater became the demand of life upon him. Wherever he tried to hide himself, whatever self-mortification he practised, life's universal agent, sex, haunted him. Hence he developed an exaggerated view of sex, its pleasures and its sinfulness. And what is significant, he fell for women more easily than ordinary men. Viswamitra, although reduced to a skeleton under a covering of matted locks, could not withstand the seductive smiles of Menaka. It is doubtful whether an ordinary man married to a girl of his choice would have had the same illusions about voluptous dancers as this naked ascetic had.

Anyway it was universally agreed in medieval times that woman was an obstacle to the greater life. Salvation by thwarting of instincts became the goal of humanity and Buddha, with his unredeemed pessimism, was hailed as the prophet of this era. Life was a continuous state of misery and the most lucky men were those who were unborn. The noble truth on which Buddha built his ethical idealism was that "birth is painful, decay is painful, death is painful, union with the unpleasant is painful, painful is the separation from the pleasant and any craving that is unsatisfied that too is painful." From this Sidhartha deduced that life as a whole was painful.

Against this painful business we can, however, array a vast army of pleasures. Joy is the reward of the mother on beholding the face of the new-born babe; out of decay and death spring forth riotous life; union with the pleasant is pleasing; separation from the unpleasant is relief; and any legitimate craving that is satisfied, that too brings contentment and happiness. It is true that all these joys are transient when viewed from the summit of eternity, but then the travail of childbirth and the headache after heavy drinking do not last through eternity. Then there are people who make light of their pains; they laugh at death. The hero finds supreme joy in death for a cause and the mother in death for her little ones. There are men, too, to whom death is a fascinating adventure.

The fact is, Sidhartha was spoiled in childhood by his doting parents who brought him up to believe that life was a continuous state of bliss, and when the young man suddenly came upon the invalid and the corpse his brain became unsettled. Had he been brought up in normal surroundings he would have had a more balanced idea of life and death and we would have been saved a philosophy of life which, though driven out of India by Sankara, has yet left a shadow of gloom over the country.

It will be found that side by side with the ascetic school there arose another religious attitude which over-emphasized and deified sex. This new thought found many adherents all over India. The spiritually minded became intoxicated with imaginary love and fell into ecstasies in the contemplation of mystic union with the Infinite. The relation between Radha and Krishna was made capital of and devotees of the Radha-Krishna cult filled India with love-songs and the debauchee found divine sanction for license. The Sakti cult made debauchery a necessary condition for salvation. The Tantrics went still farther and identified drunkenness and dissoluteness with piety.

While the religious were thus busy finding salvation, connoisseurs of pleasure, who studied woman with the object of extracting the maximum amount of pleasure out of her, were not wanting. We have an exhaustive work on this interesting subject in our *Kama Sutras*. The author was a convivial Rishi, Vatsyayana by name, and even now his authority is exploited by charlatans who trade in love-charms and lockets.

The philosophical systems, no doubt, stood cold and aloof, ascetic to the last. Popular literature, on the other hand, indulged in lascivious descriptions of Sree Krishna's vagaries with the Gopies and the indiscretions of gods and goddesses. The fierce Vedic Indra, the drinker of Soma, the wielder of the thunderbolt, the smiter of his enemies, put down his arrows and began to make fun with the Apsaries. As a fighter his value was reduced to zero and every time a bullying Asura shook a spear at him he sought the protection of Vishnu. His were not the pleasures of the chase but of the harem filled with celestial dancers.

With such merry, popular gods it was not difficult for the debauchee to find divine sanction for anything. In fact, every form of excess was permissible if it were put down to Krishna or Sakti. License was clothed in sanctity and was indulged as a legitimate means to salvation.

This was Life's reply to asceticism.

Much as we might condemn this erotic license, we cannot but admit that it was less injurious to the dignity of women than asceticism. The philosophy behind the Sakti cult was not negative as that of asceticism was, but a positive one which treated sex as the symbol of the Dual Principle, the feminine given the leading role. Among nobler adherents of the Radha-Krishna cult there were many worthy women. Mira was a conspicuous example. Her conversion of the hoary sage Rup Gosain from the doctrine of asceticism to that of love deserves special mention. She was contemptuous of asceticism. If living on water brought salvation, Mira tells us, all the fishes would go to heaven and if a vegetarian diet paved the way to Paradise, then monkeys and cattle stood a better chance of Mukti than human beings.

All told, women were treated in medieval times not as decent human beings but as goddesses or devils. And as either springs from the same source, the position of women in those times was not an enviable one.

Nor was this wave of superstition confined to India.

Subjection of Women in India

Europe suffered even more. A reference to the position of women in medieval Europe would not be out of place here if only to give us hope, knowing from what depths Europe has risen.

Jesus' affection for women brought him much notoriety and he was openly accused of associating with all sorts of women. It brought him women friends, too, who, at a time when his male disciples denounced and deserted him, went with him to the foot of the cross and even hovered round his sepulchre after he was buried. But scarcely had the echoes of the Master's footsteps died on the hillsides of the Holy Land when his disciple, Paul, the Christian Manu, revived the laws of the Pharisee and began his tirade against women. Paul tells us that young widows have damnation in their hearts. He prohibited women from speaking in public. He advised his disciples not to touch women. To weaklings, however, he recommended marriage as an alternative to fornication, because "it is better to marry than to burn." Women's hair was anathema to him and no woman was allowed to enter a place of worship without covering her head. He was the forerunner of Schopenhauer, who described women as "long of hair and short of sense."

"St. Paul's views," says Bertrand Russell, "were emphasized and exaggerated by the early Church; celibacy was considered holy and men retired into the desert to wrestle with Satan while he filled their imagination with lustful visions.

"The Church attacked the habit of the bath on the ground that everything which makes the body more attractive tends towards sin. Dirt was praised and the odour of sanctity became more and more penetrating. 'The purity of the body and its garments,' said St. Paul, 'means the impurity of the soul.' Lice were called the pearls of God and to be covered with them was an indispensable mark of a holy man."

Again, "the writings of the Fathers are full of invectives against woman. 'Woman was represented as the door of hell, as the mother of all human ills. She should be ashamed at the very thought that she is a woman; she should live in continual penace on account of the curses she has brought upon the world. She should be ashamed of her dress because it is the memorial of her fall. She should be especially ashamed of her beauty for it is the most potent instrument of the demon. Physical beauty, indeed, was perpetually the theme of ecclesiastical denunciations, though one singular exception seems to have been made; for it has been observed that in the Middle Ages the personal beauty of Bishops was continually noticed upon their tombs. Women were even forbidden by a provincial council in the sixth century, on account of their impurity, to receive the Eucharist into their naked hands. Their essentially subordinate position was continually maintained.'

"The laws of property and inheritance were altered in the same sense against women and it was only through the free-thinkers of the French Revolution that daughters recovered their rights of inheritance."*

The pious of the Middle Ages could look upon woman only as a temptress and it was gravely doubted if she had a soul. "In the council of Macon, they decided by a majority of votes that women had souls." But these souls were believed

---

* Russell: *Marriage and Morals.*

to be created for hell-fire, as any amount of punishment in this world was not considered sufficient for the sins of the fair sex. The clergy were not to have intercourse with women and for frail laymen marriage was tolerated as a legitimate form of lust. While all women were considered to be the agents of the devil, very beautiful ladies whose charms the saints could not contemplate without wicked pleasure were suspected to be Lucifer himself in disguise. Thus we have the story of the Duchess of Anjou who was such a suspect:

"Fulke, Duke of Anjou, who, notwithstanding his quarrelling propensities, was a very good Christian, took it grievously to heart that his fair consort always quitted church on the elevation of the Host; and, determined to cure her of this vagary, he one morning gave private instructions to four sturdy pages to seize her at the critical moment and hold her down by the mantle. This mandate was obeyed but the countess with her delicate scruples on the point was not to be overcome by four or even forty pages let them be as sturdy as they might. And coolly dropping her mantle into their hands, she hopped out of the church by the window leaving behind her a most suspicious odour of brimstone, which, as may be imagined, satisfactorily explained both her repugnance to the host and her precipitate disappearance."*

If such were the suspicions regarding beautiful women, those regarding ugly women were worse. Any woman with a squint or a wrinkle was suspected of being a witch. There are treatises on witches and witchcraft in which experts laid down rules for testing witches and distinguishing the true specimen. One method of ascertaining this was "by lacerating their bodies with pins three inches long." King James was

* Fullon: *History of Woman.*

85

an authority on the subject and has an essay on demonology to his credit. According to him the best method of testing a witch was to lay her full length in a pond stitched in a blanket. If she were innocent, we are told, she would die of drowning; if guilty, she would not, and then she could be taken out and burnt according to the laws of decent Christians.

All Europe, Catholic as well as Protestant, went witch-mad. "Pope Innocent VIII, alarmed at the enormous increase of persons who had dealings with the devil, appointed special inquisitors to deal with them. These men became known as the 'witch-finders.' They put each suspect on the rack and, during the torture, asked each one the same questions, the agony of pain invariably drawing out the expected replies. The inquisitors were armed with complete power to torture and to destroy, and thus exterminate as quickly as possible the crime of witchcraft. In Como alone there perished by fire one thousand persons in the year 1524, and in many other towns the burnings exceeded one hundred. The populace looked on complacently, even gladly, believing that every witch the less meant greater safety for their own children, for themselves and for their homes and prospects; though to have wept for a witch would, of course, have been at once construed into confession of the crime."*

"In course of time," to quote Fullon again, "every aged woman whom infirmity or failing years rendered cross and fretful ran the risk of being considered a witch and as such might be brought to trial and on the slightest evidence condemned and burnt. Hundreds of innocent women were accused of holding communication with the Evil One, brought to a mock trial, subjected to a barbarous and in-

* T. B. Hyslop: *The Great Abnormals.*

human ordeal and in almost every instance sentenced to be burnt."

Nor was it always the old and the infirm that suffered. The fate of Joan of Arc proves that any unconventional behaviour was sufficient cause for burning women as witches.

When kings and clergy were thus engaged in purging Christendom of witches, the laymen were busy protecting the chastity of their women. The Mediterranean Christians, due to their contact with Muslims, were ever jealous. While they demanded the utmost fidelity from their women, it could not be said that their example was such as to inspire a love of virtue in their wives. Their suspicion of their wives could be equalled only by the looseness of their own lives. And what they could not command by love they decided to extract by force. Women were watched, guards were set to spy upon them, and their freedom of movement was curtailed. But the genius of women eluded the vigilance of their husbands. They found subtle yet effective ways of committing adultery. Desperate remedies were resorted to by men to overcome this tendency. They went to the extent of inventing mechanical contrivances by means of which they tried to keep the virtue of their women under lock and key. There was widespread use of "chastity girdles," by means of which men secured the sinning parts of their wives and locked them. The ingenuity displayed in the design and construction of these girdles is worthy of a better cause. Men forced them on their women, locked them, and put the key in their pockets, then they went on business. While the merchant was soundly sleeping in the firm belief that his wife's virtue lay safely in his pocket, his wife, however, was entertaining her paramour in her bedroom, having opened the chastity belt by means of a duplicate key. Then there were tales of the girdles having been broken through "accident." A medieval bard sings in despair that it is easier to keep a swarm of fleas in a basket than to keep the virtue of a woman under lock and key.*

In proportion to the restrictions imposed upon married women did the freedom of courtesans, public dancers, and other unowned women increase. A traveller to the city of Venice in its palmy days describes it as a city of barebosomed courtesans and imprisoned wives.

The adherents of the Radha Krishna cult were represented in Europe by the troubadours and the various orders of knighthoods. The troubadour went about singing in ecstasy the praises of the mistress he had never seen and the knight travelled far out of his way to find maidens in distress who would rather have been left alone. These institutions of chivalry, no doubt, must have had their origin in the good intentions of those who thought that some sort of security was necessary for women in those turbulent times. But in their zeal for the protection of the fair, the devotees of the cult exceeded all limits. Some of the knighthoods, like the Templars, degenerated into vice and had to be massacred in cold blood. All the knighthoods developed a tendency to reduce woman to helplessness. The honour of the knight increased in proportion to the weakness of the lady he defended. Cervantes noticed this unnatural zeal of the chivalrous and gave the cult such a kick that the knight thenceforth disappeared from mature European literature except as an object of ridicule.

* Readers interested in chastity-belts may read all about them in Eric Dingwall's *Girdle of Chastity*.

Subjection of Women in India

If Cervantes and others attacked misguided chivalry, Martin Luther sounded the death-knell of asceticism in Europe. This reformer and his adherents threw open the convents and monasteries to tell the inmates that there is no virtue in celibacy, that God was likely to be pleased not with unnecessary human suffering caused by the thwarting of instincts but rather by a correct appreciation of the means of happiness he has given to mankind. Thenceforth, Europe has been steadily discarding the burdens of the past and with the added impetus of the French Revolution has now left behind all the nations of the East from whom she learnt the elements of civilization.

WIDOW-BURNING AND CHILD-MARRIAGE

Widow-burning is the Indian counterpart of European witch-burning. Some people are of opinion that this barbarous custom had its origin in husband-murder. Considering the treatment meted out to women in medieval India it is quite possible that the practice of disposing of cruel husbands by questionable means was fairly widespread. It is significant that Manu's code makes no mention of Sati. It is probable that the practice was the reaction of women towards the code. This reaction must have been violent and men must have resorted to desperate remedies.

Those who contend that Indian women have always been so sweet, gentle, and spiritual, that they could never have desired freedom from the thraldom of man by violent means, would do well to read the following casual list of Hindu kings murdered by or at the instigation of their wives:

Women and Marriage in India

"Hidden in the queen's chamber, his own brother killed king Bhadrasena; hiding himself under the bed of his mother his son killed king Karusha; mixing fried rice with poison as though with honey his own queen poisoned Kasiraja; with an anklet painted with poison his own queen killed Vairantya; with a gem of her zone bedaubed with poison his own queen killed Sauvira; with a looking glass painted with poison his own queen killed Jalutha; and with a weapon hidden under her tuft of hair his own queen slew Viduratha."*

It cannot be that the use of poison was known only to queens. The use of this subtle method of disposing of cruel husbands must have been widespread. Poison is a weapon admirably adapted to the genius of woman and even now it is often resorted to by women in India against cruel husbands. But man put an effective stop to the undesirable practice by inventing the still more undesirable institution of Sati. When a wife had to be burnt with her husband, whether she was guilty or not, no husband could be neglected, much less murdered, by a wife who loved her life. The practice thus begun as a preventive against husband-murder must have passed on to posterity as a religious duty. Arguments, too, were not wanting to sanctify it. Marriage being a mystic rite by which a woman was merged with a man for all eternity, it was not considered right to separate a wife from her husband under any circumstances whatever. Thus husbands and wives should die simultaneously and if Nature made a mistake and killed a man before his wife, it was a reasonable duty to rectify this mistake of Nature and burn the widow with her husband so that the couple may live together in the next world. If, however, the wife died before the husband, the

* Kautilya's *Arthasastra*, translated: R. Shama Shastri, p. 46.

Subjection of Women in India

latter burnt the dead body, performed the purification ceremony, and sought for a fresh virgin.

It was but natural that the Brahmin sought Vedic authority for Sati. But there was no mention of Sati anywhere in the Vedas and the Vedic widows, as we have already seen, were allowed not only to live but even to remarry. In the Rig Veda we find the following hymn:

> Rise, come into the world of life, oh! woman,
>   Come, he is lifeless by whose side thou liest;
> Wifehood with this thy husband was thy portion,
>   Who took thy hand and wooed thee as a lover.*

The words were addressed to the widow, who was wailing by the dead body of her husband, by her brother-in-law before he led her from the cremation ground to her home. Nor did the code of Manu come to the aid of the Brahmins. With all its invectives against women there is no trace in Manu's code of women being asked to destroy themselves on the funeral pyres of their husbands. Manu discourages widow marriage and decrees that a widow must spend her days in austerities and must do nothing to insult the memory of her dead husband. Beyond that he says very little about widows.

All this, however, did not stop the enterprising Brahmins from finding texts for widow-burning. In the Rig Vedic hymn xviii. 7, it is said, the word "Agre" was altered into "Agni" and this provided the desired sanction. Of this perversion of the text Max Muller says: "This is perhaps the most flagrant instance of what can be done by an unscrupulous priesthood. Here have thousands of lives been sacrificed

* Rig Veda, xviii. 8.

and a practical rebellion threatened on the authority of a passage which was mangled, mistranslated and misapplied."

Those orthodox people who believe that Sati originated in the devotion of the noble Hindu wife to her husband and her unwillingness to outlive her lord, would do well to bear in mind that they are unwittingly rejecting Manu's authority, as, according to this sage, such devotion is foreign to the nature of woman. It is true that in historical period Sati was voluntary, at least nominally; but it is more probable that in the first place it was compulsory and the modification was the result of Muslim influence. Even in historical times social pressure had the effect of compulsion. The praise attached to Saties was such that all respectable women were honour-bound to destroy themselves on the funeral pyres of their husbands. Besides, the stigma attached to widowhood and the cruel treatment meted out to the widow who did not commit Sati were such that most women chose Sati as a lesser evil than widowhood.

Nor was actual physical violence wanting in many cases. In a petition to the Governor-General for the abolition of Sati, Raja Ram Mohan Roy and his friends say:

"Your petitioners are fully aware from their own knowledge and from the authority of credible eye-witnesses that cases have frequently occurred where women have been induced by the persuasions of their next heirs interested in their destruction, to burn themselves on the funeral pile of their husbands; that others, who were induced by fear to retract a resolution rashly expressed in the first moments of grief of burning with their husband, have been forced upon the pile and there bound down with ropes and pressed with green bamboos until consumed by the flames; that, some after flying from the flames, have been carried back by their relations and burnt to death."*

In Calcutta City alone, we are told, 1,528 such wretched creatures were burnt to death between the year 1815 and 1818. Ram Mohan Roy, with his characteristic hatred of superstition, fought vigorously against this barbarity, and Lord William Bentinck stopped the practice in 1829. But our learned Pundits could not tolerate so flagrant an insult to their religion. They cried that the foundations of Hindu society would be shaken if widows were not burnt alive much in the same fashion as orthodox people at present raise an outcry at any reform. Moreover, the Pundits pretended that the abolition of widow-burning was an interference with the rights of women on the ground that the practice gave them an excellent chance of burning their sins and securing salvation straight away. They fought their case right up to the Privy Council, quoting Sastras for every argument. But, fortunately for India, the Mutiny had not yet frightened the Englishman into a cautious non-intervention, and Queen Victoria had not yet undertaken to protect all the superstitions of India. So the Privy Council rejected the petition of the Pundits and upheld the decision of Bentinck. Thus foiled, the Pundits avenged themselves by persecuting widows more than ever.

*   *   *   *   *

Another evil institution which broke Indian women was child-marriage. "A man of thirty," says Manu, "should marry a girl of twelve, a man of twenty-four a girl of eight." A girl whom her father does not give away in marriage three

* *Father of Modern India.*

years after puberty can take the law into her own hands, and look for a husband for herself. Manu does not say that it is sinful for a girl to be married after puberty, but all the later law-givers pronounce a curse on the father in whose house a daughter matures before marriage and condemn such a girl to the status of a Sudra woman. The Brahmin who marries her, we are told, descends to the level of a Sudra. As compared with these legislators Manu is a liberal law-giver.

According to Marichi, a father who gives in marriage a girl of eight attains heaven, the giver of a girl of nine Vaikunta, and one who gives his daughter before she reaches ten, attains Brahma Loka. The father of a girl married after puberty goes straight to hell. The imprecations of Parasara, who is the law specialist for Kali Yuga, on the relatives of a girl who attains puberty before marriage, although disgusting from all standards of decency, should be quoted, for they help us to understand how strongly the Rishis felt in this respect. "If a father," says he, "fails to give away his daughter in marriage when she has reached the twelfth year, her ancestors drink the blood of her menstrual flow every month. The father, mother, and elder brother of a maiden, seeing her in the menstrual course, go to hell. The Brahman who, blinded by ignorance, marries her is unfit to converse or dine with; he is the husband of a Sudra woman."*

There is a Vedic Mantra to the effect that every Aryan receives his bride from Agni after she reaches puberty. He is said to be her fourth husband, the gods Soma, Gandharva, and Agni having enjoyed her in turn before puberty. This Mantra provides an inspiration to one Rishi. According to

* Quoted from *Marriage of Brahman Girls after Puberty*, published by the Madras Hindu Association.

him the idea behind child-marriage is to rob the gods of their dues. "When hair begins to appear," says he, "Soma enjoys a maiden; when the breasts begin to grow, the Gandharva enjoys her; and when menstruation has set in, Agni is said to enjoy her. Therefore before any of these things begins to show itself, hair, breasts, or menstruation, it is best to marry a girl, for then she would not have been enjoyed by Soma and others."

We differ, however, from this explanation. It is more probable that child-marriages originated at a time when the behaviour of women was far from proper according to the masculine demands of the time. Women had to be jealously guarded and watched and everything possible had to be done that they did not go out of hand. So, before they reached the age of discretion they had to change hands, and at the first signs of puberty the husband shared her bed. Nor was it necessary to always wait for the signs of puberty. Gobhila's commentator considers that the fourth night's consummation enjoined by the Vedas must take place "though the bride be physically unfit; for it does happen," he says, "that sexual desire establishes itself before puberty, and if the husband fails to gratify it, she might do something improper."

Under such conditions, the degeneration of women was complete and their vitality reached a very low ebb indeed. But what our ancestors seem to have forgotten is that men inevitably degenerate with their women.

Of the race suicide of the Hindus committed through child-marriages A. C. Das tells us: "She (woman) was allowed no choice in the selection of her husband and she was married at an age when she was incapable of understanding the real significance of marriage and exercising her own

95

judgment and discretion. Womanhood was sacrificed at the altar of supposed social convenience and purity and out of its ashes arose a race of cabined, cribbed, confined, and delicate creatures too fragile for the propagation of life, too ethereal to be of any earthly use. With her degeneration began the degeneration of the people, which has continued down to the present times with rapid and disastrous acceleration."

Such a race could not very well hold its own against a hostile world. India paid dearly for her cruelty to mothers. The fall of India as an easy prey to medieval marauders was brought about by the degeneration of the race. In spite of the boasted prowess of the Rajputs, we have every reason to believe that the Muslims were much better soldiers than the Hindus. The ease with which Ghazni plundered India as often as he pleased tells us so. There was never an engagement which seriously threatened his progress. Those ancestor-worshippers of ours, who devoutly believe that the Kshatriyas, having come from the arms of Brahma, are invincible, would, of course, put down Muslim success to treachery and sub-terfuge. But treachery and subterfuge are a recognized part of war among Hindus, also. The wily sage, Chanakya, is an authority on organized and planned treachery and his well-known treatises on state-craft could have been studied with advantage by Machiavelli. Krishna, too, was a diplomat who believed that everything was fair in war. All this serves to show that the Rajputs were beaten by the Muslims not because they had superior military ethics but because they were inferior soldiers. And, until the rise of the Maharathas, the Hindus never challenged the supremacy of the Muslims. The Maharathas could not, of course, claim aristocratic descent like the Rajputs, but there is no doubt they made better soldiers. They were less superstitious and arrogant than the Rajputs, and believed that in matters of warfare it is the long sword that decides the victory and not tall traditions of solar and lunar ancestry.

It will be found that child-marriage was the one institution that brought about the inferiority of the Hindu to the Muslim, for in all other respects the latter persecuted woman even more than the former. The arrival of Muslims in India opens up a new phase in the subjection of woman and it is essential that we survey the Muslim influence, which was of profound influence, the evil effects of which India is still suffering.

MUSLIMS AND WOMEN

The Arabs at the time of the Prophet were mostly nomads and possessed many of the simple virtues of a nomadic race. Woman was a necessary ingrediant of camp-life and she had to take part even in tribal brawls.

Although the Arabs, too, had a matriarchal phase in their ancestry, in the days of Mohammed the position of woman was one of subordination and inferiority. The Arabs were patriarchs like the Hebrews and were much addicted to polygyny, an institution which found great favour with a people who urgently stood in need of man-power to overcome their numerous enemies.

Actuated perhaps by that hard common sense which told him that people could not accept too many revolutions at once, Mohammed did not advance much beyond his times in the matter of woman. But he had a considerable regard for her, partly inspired by his own innate sense of chivalry and

G

Women and Marriage in India

partly by Kadija's services and devotion to him. His polygyny was not one of lust, but one entered into from a sense of duty towards friends fallen in the field for the cause. When he wooed Illead, it is said she told him that she would not make him a good wife, as she was of a jealous disposition, had a son, and was no more young. Mohammed did not deny these disqualifications like a passionate lover, but proved his case by telling her that she was younger than he, that he would be a father to her son and, as for her jealousy, that he would pray to Allah to cure her of it.

Unlike many other religious teachers, Mohammed had a very human love of sexual joys and domestic happiness, but nowhere did he treat women as articles of pleasure as did his misguided followers later. Nor could the Arab of his days afford it. The richest Arab of the Prophet's days counted his wealth in camels, horses, and a few tents. Streams flowing with wine and palaces filled with houris existed only in Paradise.

But before long the Arabs changed the history of the world. With a suddenness that took the Arabs themselves by surprise, from the obscurity of the desert they poured forth armies which began to dictate terms to Byzantian emperors. The banner of Islam was carried into far places and Muslim arms swept all before them. Trade followed the flag. Wealth poured into the city of Baghdad and the desert dweller abandoned his native simplicity and took to the ways of the city. Refinements in pleasure began to be invented. Sex, the illimitable field of the pleasure-hunter, was exploited with savage enthusiasm. Byzantian and Persian vices were imported into Muslim cities and further improved. Polygyny showed its cloven hoof. Arabs began to grow tired of waiting till death for the enjoyment of Paradise. The wealthy excelled

Subjection of Women in India

Paradise itself in the number and quality of their houris. Nor was the Commander of the Faithful lacking in zeal. He counted the Circasian and Persian slave-girls of his harem in hundreds. Trading in slave-girls was the most profitable and fashionable enterprise of the time, and palatial establishments were kept by merchants where princes and nobles retired for pleasure and where seductive Greek girls ruined promising young men. Some of these singing girls were sold for fabulous sums to infatuated men.

Given this new role of a pleasure-supplier, woman began to please with a vengeance. Courtesans and dancers held the Caliph and the nobles under their thumbs. These women had no loyalty either to a country or to Islam. All they had were sweet smiles and supple bodies and they knew that these charms would vanish with youth. They made hay while yet there was sunshine. They meddled in affairs of State just to satisfy their own vanity and to impress their importance upon their rivals. A weak Caliph (and all later Caliphs, with few exceptions, were weak) easily played into their hands and they used him unscrupulously. Nor did the hold of a singing girl have any permanence about it. Every caravan brought the Caliph a cargo of beautiful girls sent in by zealous generals of newly-conquered territories and the Commander of the Faithful forgot the favourite of yesterday in the warm embrace of the new-found beauty of to-day. Nor do we feel like quarrelling with Fate when we hear that some of these zealous generals got their reward, like Cassim, the conqueror of Sind, who was sewn up in a sack and sent to Baghdad on the orders of the Caliph, given under the instigation of the very girls he sent as prizes to his master.

There is a Muslim law which gives to the sons of slave-girls right of inheritance equally with the sons of legitimate wives. Superficial commentators hold this to show the great democratic spirit of Islam. But it shows nothing of the sort. If anything, it tends to reveal the insignificance of women, a legal recognition of the superstition that the soil is of no importance and the seed is everything. Anyway, this law must have kept many a Muslim king out of his harem. Every one of the king's innumerable wives and concubines had a son or two and every mother forwarded the claims of her son to the throne, with the result that the king who retired to his harem for pleasure invited nagging and intrigue and even murder.

Lust, like the craving for drink, is incapable of satiation. The greater the indulgence, the stronger the craving. The Muslims, very soon found that even Paradise with its voluptuous houris and streams gurgling with wine could not give them satisfaction. They exhausted all the pleasures the feminine body could afford and began to exploit unnatural vice. Sodomy became the pet vice of the nobles and the well-to-do. The Commander of the Faithful often led the way. We are told by Khuda Bux, in his delightful essays *Studies Indian and Islamic*, the story of a boy who became the object of jealousy between the Caliph and his brother; the boy was shut up in the seraglio, the Caliph fearing his abduction. Nobles prided themselves on the number of boys and pages in their court as much as they did on the number of their mistresses. The "beloved" of the poets of these degenerate days was a male and not a female. The voice of the few Muslims who denounced this iniquity and yearned for the native simplicity of the Arab of the Prophet's days was drowned in the shouting of the crowd.

Subjection of Women in India

Now the most virile man cannot satisfy the sex-hunger of hundreds of idle women, much less a king or noble rendered impotent by a thousand vices. The fair captives of the harem, idling, gossiping, and carrying tales against one another, wanted some outlet for their pent-up passions. And they began freely to intrigue with slaves and courtiers. This wounded the pride of the proprietor of the harem, and he insisted, that, since he was impotent, his wives should remain chaste; death was the penalty for connexions between slaves and ladies of the harem. Yet the ingenuity of women prevailed over the laws of the Caliph; intrigues inside the harem became so scandalous that the Caliph and the nobles were more occupied with securing the chastity of their women than with securing the integrity of the empire. Then they decided to put an end to this scandal by importing eunuchs and setting them to guard the seraglio in the fashion of the Persians and Byzantian Christians. Very soon these human mules became an institution of cruelty and ferocity unparalleled even in those dark ages. But the wonder of it is, woman outwitted even the eunuchs and these themselves were implicated in criminal connexion with women.

Then there developed the cult of the veil. Although it is generally supposed that the veil was an invention for curtailing the freedom of women, it is more reasonable to suppose that the loss of freedom was the result of the veil, its object being the cultivation of certain pleasurable features. The veil, as those who have lived among people who observe it know, is capable of producing a certain type of feminine beauty, pale and passionate, with mystic eyes, and the mind of a child. Healthy, virile women, with independent mental qualities, seldom appeal to the morbid tastes of the pleasure lover. Moreover, veiled women have the attraction all hidden and mysterious things have. Freedom of social intercourse between the sexes has the effect of toning down the sexual impulses, and the Muslim of the later days was not willing to forgo his pleasures. Hence his inauguartion of the veil, making a mystery of women.

Those who see in the veil an exclusive instrument for curtailing feminine freedom would note that Muslim traditions and laws are generally more liberal than Hindu, and that early Muslim and pre-Islamic Arabs had very little of the veil. It was not so much the freedom of women the later Muslim opposed as the loss of feminine charm through freedom. Women for them were essentially objects of pleasure and if freedom and outdoor life interfered with feminine charms so much the worse for feminine freedom and outdoor life. The idea is real enough to many even to-day when it is said that the modern girl loses her attractions through tennis and advanced education.

In the earlier days of the veil high-spirited women revolted against it. Ayesha (a niece of Ayesha, wife of the Prophet) never wore the veil, although her husband insisted. "On me," said she, "God has set the seal of beauty and I rejoice when my beauty is seen and the mercy of God therein acknowledged. Never shall I cover my face, for no flaw or fault finds a place in God's work." (Khuda Bux.) But women of this spirit were few, their voices were heard only in the earlier days of Islam and men did not find them difficult to suppress.

Nor did theologians fail to take note of the levity of the fair sex. In the early days of Islam, women went out when they pleased and enjoyed with men the right of praying in the mosque. This practice, however, was later found to be most objectionable to Allah and it had fallen into disrepute by the third century A.H. Considering the erotic pitch of the later Muslims, it is good that women were kept from the mosque; otherwise the house of God might have become something quite otherwise.

"The disgrace of having lowered the position of women," says Khuda Bux, "belongs in the first place to the morose fanatical theologians of Islam. It was not due, to be sure, to the fact that they were indifferent or insensible to feminine charms—for they had their own well-stocked harems—but outside that little Paradise they loved to affect a thorough contempt for things of the world and the levity of the fair sex. For this reason, perhaps, one of the oldest traditionalists had collected, with apparent relish, several traditions which purport to say that women for the most part will go to hell."

Muslim women, no doubt, had gone to hell, thanks to the perversity of men. But they dragged men with them, and this the traditionalist does not seem to have noticed. It was not long before the once-invincible Muslim world lay prostrate at the feet of the Mongol and the Christian.

It was this degraded moral code of an Islam fallen from its original purity that Muslims brought to India to fill the cup of misery. The newcomers had nothing in common with the natives except this love of persecuting women. In the first days of hatred, the Hindus and the Muslims each prided themselves that their own laws for the subjection of women were the best and each refused to learn from the other. But in due time, the Hindus, in the manner of all conquered races, began to imitate their masters. Hindu princes, nobles, and merchants improved their Zenanas in Muslim fashion and elaborate precautions were taken to safeguard women from prying eyes when the "Zenana" moved about. Middle-class women, as far as possible, stayed at home, but when they had to move abroad they covered their faces. If the Hindu did not sew up veils like the Muslim it was not because he wanted his women to be more free, but because he had a hatred of tailors. He clearly enough caught the spirit of the veil, and he achieved its end without incurring the tailor's bill by making his wife put the Sari over her head, so that it might be pulled down across her face. This Sari-cum-veil is, in fact, a more barbarous instrument than the veil proper, in the same way as killing with a blunt chopper is more cruel than killing with the edge of a sharp sword. The veil proper has at least the advantages of efficiency. It has eye-holes and a proper support at the crown of the head and its blankness is much relieved by artistic embroidery. None of these advantages can be claimed for the Sari-cum-veil. A woman moving in it looks like a corpse wriggling out of death, whereas one that moves in the veil proper looks only like a ghost in search of its lost grave.

*   *   *   *   *

Those brave men and women who fight for the emancipation of Indian women have to fight against overwhelming odds. They have to fight Manu, the Caliph, the Mullah, the Pundit, the prince, and the sturdy wife-beating peasant, to say nothing of the vast army of conventional moralists.

In spite of the great disabilities of Muslim women which are apparently more degrading than those of Hindu women, the reformer would find it more difficult to emancipate

Subjection of Women in India

Hindu than Muslim women. The degradation of Muslim women is more superficial than vital. The Muslim is, after all, a blunt fellow and it does not take much brains to prove his iniquities. He is never given to too much imagination. His methods of achieving ends are direct. When he set to reducing his wife to his will, he shut her up in a room and kept a watch over her. He did not take pains to teach her the glories of solitary confinement. He is a bad diplomat. This is amply proved by the attitude of some of our Muslim League leaders who began as diplomats and soon degenerated into bullies. The Muslim is not yet schooled to the art of subtlety and suggestion. His wife remains a rebel inside the veil. Her vitality is not reduced by child-marriage* and religious suggestion. In fact, the rigour of the veil proves the intensity of the rebellion within. The aggressiveness of the Muslim is a manifestation of the pent-up fury of his mother.

But the case of the Hindu is different. The methods of the Brahmin in gaining his ends are essentially subtle and far-reaching. The difference between the Hindu and the Muslim in methods of conquest can best be illustrated by a comparison of the treatment each of them meted out to conquered races. When the Muslims conquered India they were contemptous of the Hindus and their religion, broke their idols and plundered their temples, invited them to embrace Islam if they wished to be saved, and massacred those who refused.

* Though by no means general, child-marriages are found existing also among the Muslims of India. Not only in places where Hindu influence is predominant, but even in Sind where Muslim sway has been complete and continuous from the days of the first Muslim onrush, we find, in certain Muslim families, children of five and six being married; another proof of the subtle powers of Hinduism for conquering its conqueror.

Women and Marriage in India

The conquered races were left under no delusions as to their humiliations. But when the Indo-Aryans subdued the then natives of India, these were cajoled into the belief that it was a privilege to be kicked by an Aryan. They treated the conquered as less than beasts by pronouncing them as unapproachables and untouchables; but the Sudra and the Panchama were taught that slavery to their superiors was a religious duty, by the scrupulous exercise of which they might become as good as the Brahmin himself in an after-life. Hence we find that when later the Muslims extended their religious fellowship towards the untouchable and the unapproachable, these were found to be as much against their own uplift as the Brahmin. Again, witness the ardour with which the Dravidians of the south read the *Ramayana*, a work in which the right half of their ancestors are described as demons and the other half as monkeys.

This subtle method of subjugation applies in the matter of women as well. To subject women to the will of man, the Hindus invented a literature that tells of wives who performed every kind of unnatural action for the sake of their husbands, and enunciated a cult of husband-worship which was set up as the only way of salvation for women. The result is, Hindu women find a morbid pleasure in their slavery, hope to be kicked to heaven by their husbands, are content to live as appendages to men and oppose freedom with even greater fanaticism than men. Even women of education, who ought to know better, wail over the ancient heroines of India who worked miracles by their powers of Pathivrityam, and the degeneration of the modern girl. But the ancient heroines, it must be remembered, existed only in the imagination of poets who lived mainly on roots and leaves in the jungle.

Subjection of Women in India

Enough has now been said to convince the reader of the miserable condition of Indian women, whether Hindu or Muslim, although much remains unsaid. A general line of uplift is suggested in the following chapters; details are left to better hands.

CHAPTER III

Emancipation of Women

★

THE suggestion of emancipating women fills many men with a nightmare vision of licentious women running amuck in a society of sober men, divorcing husbands, breaking up homes, neglecting children, and sinning in the open street. This profound misconception of woman as a wicked animal with no intelligence or common sense was never more brazenly betrayed by men than in the days of the suffrage movements of New Zealand and Europe.

Women's suffrage was prophesied to be the beginning of anarchy. Men were afraid that their wives would grab political power, turn all the man-made laws of the country upside down and reduce man to a state of dependence on woman. The fact that in all the countries that agitated for women's suffrage the female population is greater than the male aggravated this fear and turned it into a panic. Besides, the treatment meted out to their wives and daughters by men all down the centuries was not such as to inspire confidence in a State dominated by women.

From New Zealand came the prediction that "one of the fairest spots on earth was going to be turned into a howling wilderness by women's suffrage." Those who were in the confidence of the Almighty assured the New Zealanders that

Emancipation of Women

women's suffrage was "contrary to the ordinance of God." Some gentlemen were of opinion that the New Zealanders "would probably be for some years to come a dreadful object lesson to the rest of the British Empire."

Even level-headed Englishmen got seriously alarmed when their women began to agitate for the right to vote. A certain English judge raised a queer legal point when a lawyer defending a lady-client's right to vote, maintained that her name was already entered in the voters' list and a name once entered could not be struck off. His Lordship wanted to know if a dog had a right to vote if its name got into the voters' list. Another Briton thought that women's suffrage was too bold an experiment to be begun by Englishmen. "This is an experiment," said he, "so large and bold that it ought to be tried by some other country first." He was apparently waiting to see France or Sweden ruined by women politicians and then tell the world what he thought of women.*

Such were the predictions of gloomy prophets about the results of women's suffrage and such the distrust of women prevalent even in countries where they have shown their capabilities in every direction. Subsequent events, however, have given the lie to all these predictions. Women of Great Britain, at present, could capture all the seats of the House of Commons, if they wanted to, form a cabinet of women, and turn the laws of the country upside down. But they have sufficient common sense to know that centuries of tradition cannot be changed in a day. Women are more conservative

* Those who wish to read more of these calamitous predictions can read them in M. Faucett's interesting little book, *Women's Suffrage*, from which the quotations above are taken.

than men and they stick to the accepted order of things even when it is unfavourable to them, because of their instinctive dread of revolution in which women are likely to suffer more than men. Besides, they know that wranglings in parliaments, fighting and killing one another in the name of patriotism and imperialism, bullying, spying, carrying tales on an international scale, in short, all the hypocrisy and cruelty that go by the name of government, war, and diplomacy, are best left to men.

In India, men's distrust of women is more pronounced and crude than in European countries. The medieval heritage of sex-slavery is so deeply ingrained that they instinctively revolt at the very thought of sex-equality. And where prejudice is so strong there can be no scarcity of arguments. The confusion prevailing in the matter of women's legal and political rights, even in the minds of well-educated Indians, is such that a clear statement of the case is necessary.

SEX-EQUALITY

Demands for legal or political equality of treatment for the sexes do not involve an assumption that men and women are alike or that men are capable of bearing children. Men and women are not alike any more than Jawaharlal and Jinnah, Gandhi and C. V. Raman, Subhas Chandra Bose and Sapru, Bhai Parmanand and Sreenivasa Sastri, Abdul Gaffoor Khan and Moonje, are alike. All these men differ widely from one another; and in the one sex may be found even psychological, if not biological, freaks who are unsexed or under-sexed while possessing, to all outward appearances, the marks of the

Emancipation of Women

male. But that does not prevent us from treating all the famous, as well as the millions of other less conspicuous countrymen of ours, alike, politically and legally.

Those who harp on the superiority of the male as an argument against political and legal equality of women with men suffer from a curious illusion that in our society people are treated by law each according to his merit. If we are to presume that this is so, we will be driven to the quaint conclusion that in matters of managing inherited wealth, Sarojini Naidu and Vijay Laxmi Pundit are at present moving on a lower plane of intelligence than the male village idiot.

Democracy is not a form of government which guarantees to treat each according to his merit. No form of government would try to do a thing so preposterous. If anything, democracy tends to guarantee equality of treatment to the fool and the genius alike.

Advocacy of equal rights of treatment by law does not involve a blindness to the existence of manifested superiority, inferiority, and difference. It is based on a doctrine of potential equality. The doctrine may be wrong; but it is the most practical method of ensuring fairplay to the majority in the community. It may be true, for example, that Pundit Jawaharlal Nehru has the right of a hundred thousand votes if we take the worth of the political opinion of the average Indian as the unit. But with all our admiration for the Pundit, we cannot let him vote a hundred thousand times as, in that case, we will be confronted with the impossible task of deciding the individual political worth of every Indian relative to an average and drawing our voters' list accordingly. And so, as practical politics, we give our distinguished countryman the right of a single vote thus bringing him down to the level of the street loafer and the tea-shop gossip.

Not only theories of democratic government, but all the great religions of the world, are founded upon theories of potential equality of the ego (they may call it soul) and on a refusal to admit the bewildering variations so obvious to the naked eye.

If apparent superiority is the justification for the tyranny of man to woman why should we not apply it to nations as well? Nobody but the hopelessly prejudiced would deny that the average twentieth-century Englishman is a superior animal to the average Indian. As such, on what grounds does the Indian aspire to freedom and equality of treatment with the Englishman?

The Indian aspires to freedom and equality of treatment on theories of potential equality with the Englishman. We Indians believe that it is not because of any inherent superiority in the ego of the Englishman that he rules India, but that the conditions of centuries are responsible for his having been able to obtain mastery over our country. We believe that the personality of the Indian never had a chance to express itself in the British period and that our talents are lying dormant; and we prove our contention by a reference to the past wherein our ancestors were bigger bullies than Englishmen. We do not believe, like the European, that all Asiatics are barbarians, but we believe that the Asiatics are as good as Europeans and that if the former lag behind in certain aspects of progress external influences are responsible. And now that the Japanese have proved that they can be as ruthless in commercial competition as Britishers and Americans, and as cold-blooded as Italians in bombing women and children, Westerners are beginning to believe that the Asiatics are capable of civilization.

*   *   *   *   *

The present inferiority of women in fields of activities common to both sexes is an artificial one brought about by centuries of oppression. Work and freedom of movement for women did not fit in with medieval theories of morality, and in course of time women of "good breeding" became incapable of doing any work except back-biting, assuming superior airs, making a nuisance of themselves, and generally wasting the earnings of honest workers. And, since, according to Darwin, women have a tendency to transmit feminine traits to daughters and men masculine traits to sons, each generation of Indian women began to produce a worse generation of daughters, with the result that to-day we have our country infested with ugly, stupid, unhealthy, undesirable women, especially among the middle classes.

If Indians really believe in the honour and prudence of their women, they should prove it not by calling them Devi, Devi, and treating them like slaves, but by calling them by their proper names and treating them like reasonable human beings. Women's status in society should be made such that the birth of a daughter should be looked upon as welcome to the family and not as a domestic calamity.

Now that we have abolished the slavery of man to man and are none the worse for it, it is time we abolished the slavery of woman to man and recognized her as his equal in every respect. At the start of the movement to abolish slavery, we all know, people of great wisdom predicted calamity for mankind. It was impossible to run the world

without slaves, they asserted. America had even to fight a
civil war to prove that it is possible to run the world without
slaves, if we took pains enough. Now we know that the
abolition of slavery has made the world a better place to live
in both for the slave and the slave-driver. Similarly, those
prophets who predict ruin for a world of emancipated women
would be pleasantly surprised to find that free women make
better wives than slave-women.

MATCH-MAKING

No human institution is perfect; and marriage being the
most vital of all human institutions, is perhaps the most
imperfect. Its very sanctity proclaims its imperfections. The
nervous recital of Mantras, the feasting and rioting, the
tumult and the shouting, the chanting of hymns and the
beating of drums, are all desperate attempts to drown the
misery of the sorry affair. But this is hardly the way to solve
a difficult problem. If we take some pains to understand the
problem and throw off the yoke of tradition, we can make
marriage an institution tolerable enough for decent human
beings to live in without indulging in this sort of African
witchcraft.

The knotty part of the matrimonial problem is to decide
upon a guiding principle which would lead us to happy
marriages. The present method of parents arranging matches
without consulting the participants is tantamount to forcing
promiscuity on beings endowed with discriminating faculties.
Anyway, its folly is obvious to all intelligent Indians and
need not be discussed here.

Swami Dayanand has what the Arya Samajists call an ideal

Emancipation of Women

solution to the matrimonial problem. According to him, the sexes are to be taught apart, boys by men and girls by women. The young ones thus grow up in purity. When girls reach the ideal age of sixteen and the boys twenty-four, the teachers of the schools exchange photographs of eligible candidates and compare notes. In Swamiji's own words:

"When boys and girls become of a marriageable age, when only six or twelve months are left in completion of their Brahmacharya and education, let the photographs or pictures of boys be sent to teachers of girls' schools and those of girls to teachers of boys' schools.

"Let the teachers then send for the diaries of those who are alike in outward appearance and study them carefully. When they find any two students (one male and the other female) resemble each other in disposition, temperament, character, and accomplishments and consider them suited to each other for marriage, let them place the photo and diary of the one in the hands of the other and ask them to inform them of their intentions. If they be quite willing to marry each other, let the 'return-home' ceremony of both be performed simultaneously. They should be allowed to converse with each other or hold a discussion (on any subject to test each other's knowledge and ability) in the presence of their tutors, parents, and other respectable people."

"It should be borne in mind," Swamiji warns us, "that the bride and the bridegroom should not before marriage be allowed to meet each other in retirement, since such a meeting of young people may lead to bad consequences."*

Swami Dayanand was one of our recent great men who gave India a new courage and a great hope. His revolt

* *Satyartha Prakash.*

against traditions, his hatred of idolatory, his supreme contempt for Pauranics, and his masterly art of rejecting as
spurious such portions of the scriptures as do not fit in with
our standards and interpreting others to suit our own times
all fill us with admiration for his courage and his genius.
But we would be dishonouring our modern Rishi if we
accept without question all his injunctions; for he himself
in his introduction to *Satyartha Prakash* asks us to "keep
an open mind, enter into the spirit of the author and form
an independent opinion" about his comments.

Now we shall examine how far Dayanand's injunctions
are practicable and whether it is advisable to follow them.

Swami Dayanand was a celibate and hence his treatment
of sex problems is scholarly but not realistic. His description
of the ideal sex-act, although minute as to detail, is merely
academic. His ascetic insistence on the abstinence of the
husband and wife from the time of the wife's conception till
parturition and the woman ready for another child betrays a
profound ignorance of the biological necessity of the normal
adult male; he makes a generalization of humanity, taking
himself as the normal. Above all, he overlooks the supreme
fact that sex has two different functions, the procreative
function and the play function, the latter being as important
as the former for the well-being of mankind.

These photographic marriages remind one of the bad
old days when kings used to send out the portraits of their
daughters to neighbouring kingdoms in search of sons-in-
law. What we want is the marriage of young men and women
and not of their photographs; any attempt at tying them
down by parents and teachers on the merits of photographs
and diaries is doomed to fail. Even supposing that our photo-

Emancipation of Women

graphers are capable of taking a presentable likeness of the originals, we can never know a person by a photograph. As for the debates arranged in presence of elders, we can rest assured that a girl brought up in strict seclusion is not likely to evoke the best from her future lord. The whole thing betrays an ascetic's distrust of youth.

Dayanand's injunction that teachers should select boys and girls of similar tastes as possible couples is another error arising from his lack of amorous experience. Love that arises out of similarity is often mere affection. Many great loves come from the attraction of opposites. We find men of intellect are often attracted by women of low intellectual power. Mohammed, the mystic and military genius, was fascinated by the childish vagaries of Ayesha. Handsome men fall for homely women and fair Desdemonas take to swarthy Moors. Sultana Reziah sold her kingdom for an Abyssinian slave. Jehangir, the least capable of the Great Moghuls, adored Nurjehan, famous in history for administrative ability.

Thus we find true love based upon the most unexpected combinations and which looks blind and unreasonable to those who are not a party to it. It may be that this apparent blindness of love is the result of a sound plan of Nature, by means of which she tries to equalize the disparity of the parents in the personality of the coming child. Therefore, neither parents nor teachers should interfere with men and women in their love affairs. Only the parties concerned, you may call them victims if you like, can know whom they love and whom they love not. In other words, we cannot make people love "according to plan."

As compared with this ideal of match-making by photo-

117

Women and Marriage in India

graph, we must admit the present system of parents arranging marriages has its good points. Teachers have but a schoolish interest in children and they know more of the children's ignorance than their virtues. That is why schoolboys condemned by teachers as dunces very often emerge quite successfully in later life. The relation between a child and its parent is much more intimate than that between a teacher and a pupil and hence a parent is much more qualified to make out suitable matches for young men and women. Besides, the teachers who handle the photographs are likely, if they happen to be widows, widowers, or sinners, to linger over attractive ones—to the detriment of the young candidates' claims.

It must be remembered, too, that Swami Dayanand lived in the nineteenth century and India is progressing so rapidly to-day that ideas considered revolutionary in those days have become old-fashioned in the twentieth century. By the time the modern teachers receive the photographs of the girl and the boy in question, it is likely that the young people have met already in schools, congress processions, or picture houses and talked and jested with each other, or even taken matters further.

There is an opinion in certain circles that teachers and students can be brought into perfection by going back to the Guru Kula system of education of our forefathers. In this connexion I cannot do better than quote the late Lala Lajpatrai. Speaking of the Guru Kula system, he says:

"It is extremely doubtful if the system of education advocated in the codes was ever followed universally. I have reason to think that it was mainly designed for the children of the Brahmins. However, be that as it may, I have no doubt that it is impossible for it to be reintroduced as a part of the general scheme of education in the India of to-day. I am also positive that it is detrimental to the sort of character we want to develop, nay, which we must develop in our boys and girls, if we want to keep pace with the rest of the world in their onward march. Our boys and girls must not be brought up in hot-houses. They should be brought up in the midst of society of which they are to be members. They should form habits and learn manners which would enable them to rise to every emergency. They should learn to rise above temptations and not to shun them. The world is a temptation. It is a place to enjoy as long as by doing so one does not injure oneself and others."

"As to the Dharma Sastra," he says again, "I must say that however desirable it may be for us to be acquainted with our own laws and social sciences, the current treatises are full of crude, absurd, inconsistent, diametrically antagonistic views and theories. We cannot afford to tax the mental capacity of our children by placing in their hands the current editions of Manu, Narada, and Apastambha without subjecting them to major operations."*

So much for going back to the Guru Kula system and the Dharma Sastras.

Having thus disposed of Dayanand's photographic guide to marriage, we have yet to deal with the superstition that obtains among a large percentage of Hindu population to the effect that horoscopes would lead us to ideal marriages. It is taken for granted that the planets wield a mysterious influence over the destiny of individuals and that their position in the heavens at the time of the birth of the child decides

---

* *Problem of National Education in India.*

its fate. Men who can interpret this influence are supposed to know which couples are destined to marry each other as sanctioned by the heavenly bodies.

Astrology has become the haven of all charlatans, medicine-men and necromancers after easy money and cheap fame among the ignorant. The number of these human parasites that prey upon the credulous is alarming. Almost all Hindu marriages are arranged after consulting astrologers; and the stupendous number of child-widows, orphans, and fruitless unions among the Hindus ought to convince sensible men of the futility of the horoscope as a guide to matrimony. But superstition is the negation of reason and the very failings of the matrimonial system are pointed out as proof of the incorrect usage of horoscopes. Many a promising union is wrecked on the position of Mars interpreted by ill-paid, interested, or whimsical astrologers!

Astrology is not a recognized science. To state that the position of planets has certain effects on the earth as a whole, that anything that affects the earth need necessarily have a corresponding effect on its citizens and to deduce from these premises that an astrologer can read in the position of planets an intelligent principle as to the destiny of each individual, is to give superstition the dignity of a science. True, super-stition is a relative term and it is extremely difficult to draw the line between it and faith. A belief in a personal deity, for example, is as much superstition to the atheist as black magic or African witchcraft is to the Christian and the Muslim. But then a belief is to be judged by its utility for effecting personal and social integrity.

Astrology flourishes on probabilities and the age-old human passion for prophecy. Vagueness is the strong point

Emancipation of Women

of all astrological predictions. Out of the numerous probable things they predict something does happen which, by stretching the possible meanings of the cautiously worded predictions, can be construed as having been foretold. And these are paraded with great gusto for the edification of astrology and black magic. Ordinary men and women have short memories and they forget all the predictions that did not come to pass.

It may be recalled that a certain astrologer is credited with having predicted the abdication of Edward VIII. It is significant that people knew about the existence of this prediction only after the abdication. I have read the prediction. Its wording is such that it might mean anything including an abdication. Nobody had the patience, moreover, to hunt up all the predictions this astrologer had made about King Edward and others and tell us how many of them have come true or, better still, how many of them are yet to be fulfilled. I, for one, remember a hundred predictions made by world-famous predictors and published in the daily papers which never came to pass. The defeat of Italy in Abyssinia was predicted in the same year that Mussolini annexed Abyssinia. Gandhiji spent in prison the whole year in which his release was predicted. It must be borne in mind, however, that, if Gandhi's release were predicted every year of his prison-life, the astrologer or medicine-man who happened to predict it in the right year might claim for himself the gift of prophecy, and the majority of human beings who dearly love the miraculous would proclaim him as the prophet and seer of India. Every year world-wars, earthquakes, and revolutions are predicted. Sometimes these things happen and sometimes they do not. All of which leaves us where we were. The point to be noted is that astrology, so unreliable in all other respects, cannot be expected to lead to happy marriage.

With all that, however, men and women must marry and multiply. And the only guide we can trust is love. Love alone can lead us to tolerably happy marriage.

LOVE'S GUIDANCE

While the object of Nature in making men and women mate is to multiply the race, her means of achieving this end is sexual love. Hence, the best method to beget desirable children is to follow the lead of love.

Our ancestors knew as well as we know that the proper guide for marriage is love. They knew well that in arranging marriages it is vital to take into account the feelings of the parties concerned. But if feelings or opinions are to be taken into account, they should have some maturity about them and for this it is necessary that people should marry only after they have passed adolescence at least into full youth. Then comes a period from the first signs of puberty to the marriageable age, which is a time wherein girls may go astray. Young women brought up by irresponsible parents are likely to get into trouble in this period of their lives. The correct remedy lies in the restraining influence of a proper education and in parents taking the girls into their confidence. Above all, the behaviour of parents themselves should be such as to set an example of restraint and straightforwardness to their daughters. All this involves responsibility. But our ancestors generally shouldered their responsibility by destroying it. They solved the knotty problem by introducing child-

Emancipation of Women

marriage, which curbed all independent feminine spirit and made it impossible for any girl to go astray.

For the success of love-marriages in India, the following three conditions should be fulfilled first: (1) Raising of the marriageable age, (2) the creation of a generation of lovable boys and girls, and (3) giving young men and women sufficient opportunities to meet and fall in love.

1. RAISING OF THE MARRIAGEABLE AGE is a necessity, because very young people know not what love is. The development of adolescence is a prelude to tumultuous emotions and the boy or girl hardly knows what he or she wants. When our high-school girls and boys imagine themselves to be soulfully in love, the majority of them might be merely suffering from sex hunger. Romantic literature promotes the illusion. The fact that a young man feels like crossing the seven seas, going to the ends of the earth, committing a murder or writing bad poetry does not at all mean that he is in love with the girl for whose sake he feels like performing all these strange acts. A famished man may feel just as desperate for a decent meal without necessarily having any amorous feelings towards the chicken he thinks of eating.

Sex, in its purely physical aspect, should be treated as a sort of hunger without love for the object of its gratification. Biologists tell us that very often in the jungle the female of certain carnivora perish with the sex-act. They put down the coyness of our maidens to a subconscious fear of danger inherited from their mothers of the jungle to whom love-making was a perilous adventure. This theory of masculine agressiveness is, however, amply balanced in Nature by the lethal voluptuousness of the spider and the queen bee, whose

Women and Marriage in India

lovers seldom survive their first love-making; and this perhaps accounts for the shyness of some of our young men. Kissing, they say, is an evolved form of biting; in ancient Egypt, they had only one word for both. Love-making among many animals and among some human beings is still a miniature battle. I would not revolt my readers by asking them to draw conclusions from their bedroom experiences, but would rather ask them if they ever took kindly to the nocturnal amours of cats.

It is essential that young men and women, before they enter into matrimony, must be able to distinguish whether they are in love or merely groping in the dark for the unattainable. It is essential, too, that they must know the limitations of love and marriage. Love has its consequences and these are not always pleasant. Nobody who has seen a woman in an advanced state of pregnancy, no woman who has experienced the pangs of childbirth, would say that married love is a continued state of bliss. It is only fair to the young that they must be well advised in the responsibilities and shortcomings of domestic life as well as in its joys and pleasures. Many young men and women fed on romantic ideas of love enter into matrimony with extravagant hopes and they are disillusioned or even revolted in the very first days of their married life. This sort of illusion should not be encouraged if we are to advocate love-marriage. Love-marriage would not lead men and women to perfect bliss. Nothing in the world would.

The raising of the marriageable age by the Sarda Act, while it is good enough to spite our ancestors, is not good enough to lead us to a sound generation of men and women. For one thing, the Act does not extend to the native states.

Emancipation of Women

For another, the marriage ceremony performed in violation of the Act is valid even if those who conduct it may be prosecuted. Again, the penalties attached to the violation of the Act are so trifling that parents would rather face them than violate the admonition of Manu and Parasara and risk eternal damnation. Above all, the inadequacy of the Act lies in its minimum age. A girl does not attain maturity of head, heart, or body at the age of fourteen.

That girls can be depended upon to lead a life of self-restraint in sexual matters if we give them proper education is proved by our college and high-school girls, who have better discipline over themselves than girls brought up in conventional homes under the protection of the veil. I know that our moralists are up in arms against the modern girl. But the moralist's war on the modern girl is not a proof of her levity but a betrayal of the shallowness of his brains. The sins of the modern girl are more apparent than real and they get wide publicity, whereas the misdeeds of the Purdah woman rot behind the veil. And conventional moralists do not object so much to immorality as to the mention of it. They can overlook love-affairs between servants and mistresses, abortions, and the murder of young girls who cannot account for the increasing circumference of their waistbands, provided these things are done in a decent, respectable sort of way without neighbours getting to know. But if a high-school girl were caught joking with a young man on the tennis court, the elders are scandalized and write long articles to newspapers, bemoaning the degeneration of modern youth and the evils of what they call Western education and longing for the good old days of our ancient Rishies wherein every girl was a goddess and every student a true Brahmachari who never entertained woman in thought, word, or deed. It is high time this came to an end.

True, the vast majority of Indians cannot afford to send their children to college to keep them out of mischief. But they have their various occupations in which children may be asked to help. The peasant has the labours of the field, and the artisan works at home. Girls can be profitably engaged in knitting, weaving, tailoring, and a thousand other things. Marketing and social calls promise other ways of keeping girls busy. Social intercourse with a little broadmindedness can be made a pleasurable affair instead of an embarrassing one as it is understood at present. Our potentialities are many; only the will is lacking.

2. THE CREATION OF A GENERATION OF LOVABLE BOYS AND GIRLS is as important for the success of love matches as the raising of the marriageable age. At present, a good-looking girl is such a desideratum in India that when one of them happens to step into the street, the whole traffic is paralysed by those stopping to stare at her, not excluding the policeman on traffic duty. Boys by their outdoor habits, by their increased love of games (a love for which we owe eternal gratitude to the Britisher), and better facilities for social intercourse, are rapidly overcoming the accidents of birth and are increasing their physical fitness. But not so the girls. For them physical fitness is condemned as immodesty and moving about as a sort of prostitution. If a girl walks vigorously or laughs with the freedom of a healthy mind, we immediately put her down as a flirt. A girl should not run; that spoils our aesthetic sense. If she should walk at all, she must just float about in an ethereal sort of way. Conventional theories of feminine locomotion tell us that the ideal girl

Emancipation of Women

moves about majestically like an elephant or shuffles along like a swan. A life of activity and energy is unwomanly. These idiotic ideas of feminine modesty are responsible for all the ill-health of our middle-class women. They put on fat before they pass out of girlhood and are unable to move about without the help of a horse or a Ford engine. The average middle-class woman brings forth her children in infinite pain and a single delivery makes her old and anaemic. An open-air walk invariably results in influenza or a cold. And with bad health she develops a bad temper. With the loss of her natural attractions she begins to crave for ornaments. Her bodily defects she tries to hide by means of expensive Sarees, and she plagues her husband for the wherewithal to buy finery.

The proper cure for women's craze for ornament lies in giving them opportunities to acquire natural charms. Give a woman a sound mind in a sound body and she would drop her craze for jewellery. Women have a keener sense of beauty than men and if men cannot afford them opportunity to develop natural charm, they ask for artificial attractions to the embarrassment of their menfolk.

Women being the more important factor in reproduction than men, they require better physical training than men. Better does not, however, mean more vigorous. Nor need we go about inventing new games for women. They can play all the games of men with advantage. Although competing with men in games requiring physical exertion would do them no good, they can play tennis, football, hockey, and even cricket among themselves. Nor would boxing and wrestling do them any harm so long as they compete only with their own sex. But the present-day tendency of identifying beauty with incapability of motion should be completely abandoned.

For raising the capacity to enjoy life and for their physical well-being, all girls should be taught dancing. Dancing is the expression of the rhythm of life. The gestures, the movements, and the poise of a girl who has caught the rhythm of life, the way she talks or does little things are all a joy to her as well as to the beholder.

Most people will have noticed the difference in walking between an Indian and a European. To the latter walking is a rhythmic art which apparently comes without effort; but the former just tries to hobble along as best he can and reach his miserable destination as quickly as possible. This difference may in part be attributed to the Indian's apathy towards dancing and the European's love of it. It must also be said that the European walks faster than the Indian although the exertion is less apparent. It is not only in little things that rhythm counts. In all the major activities of life from the battlefield to the pulpit, rhythm is essential for success.

A love of rhythm is inborn in men and women. Children dance on hearing music with broad rhythm. All men and women are unconsciously carried away to keeping time to a good song. This innate human love of rhythm, if not controlled would run riot into the devil-dances of savages. If stifled, it will create morose type of men who do incalculable harm to their fellow-beings under the pretext of guiding their religious and moral impulses. These men have already done enough harm to India. Our philosophers have persuaded us to treat dancing with contempt and condemn it to harlots and Deva Dasies. How even the philosophers could bring about this attitude towards the art of dancing

Emancipation of Women

remains a mystery, considering the fact that most of our gods and goddesses dance away merrily through eternity. Anyway, condemning dancing to the brothel has brought about the ruin of many an innocent lover of music and rhythm. Love-making is essentially rhythmic and the static stupidity of a wife very often drives a lover of rhythm to the embraces of the professional dancer. However beautiful a woman might look, if she hasn't caught the rhythm of life she is sure to prove a dull sexual partner.

And what applies to women, applies with equal force to men.

Physical beauty is, to a large extent, a matter of proportion, and health goes a long way in deciding the correctness and symmetry of human proportions. Women, just like men, need fresh air, exercise, games, work, and social intercourse for their physical well-being. If you shut a woman up in a room she becomes pale and sickly; if you under-feed her she dies of under-nourishment; if you strike her she feels pain; if you force her obedience she resents it; and if you thwart her instincts she revolts against your tyranny. In short, if Indians treat their women as they are treating them to-day, they will not succeed in creating a generation of lovable women. If, on the other hand, they treat them like human beings and not as valuable property liable to be stolen or damaged on exposure, there would be no difficulty in creating a new generation of desirable women with whom men can make love and contract matrimonial alliances without invoking the aid of gods and demons.

3. GIVING YOUNG MEN AND WOMEN OPPORTUNITIES TO FALL IN LOVE. This, no doubt, is a difficult problem fraught with many dangers. But we must face these dangers with

courage whatever be the risks involved. Other countries of the world have found out a working solution, and there is no reason why India should not try her best.

The introduction of co-education has opened up great possibilities for love-marriages. In New India there should not be separate schools for boys and girls. For subjects which have to be taught to each sex separately, say, for example, motherhood or fatherhood, periods may be set apart for separate study. The present-day seating arrangements should also be changed, as the segregation of the sexes makes them unnecessarily sex-conscious.

Co-education is not only good social reform but wise economy. Every city in India duplicates its educational work by running separate institutions for boys and girls.

In spite of the adverse comments of those who never had the advantages of co-education, the opinion of professors and teachers who actually run the institutions is in favour of co-education. They say the students develop better manners and have better self-restraint when attending mixed classes. Youngsters, too, are very often cured of romantic obsessions. A girl who gets her ears boxed by an old-fashioned schoolmaster and weeps or blushes, might rouse feelings of sympathy or chivalry in a boy; but it is not likely that he would think of her any more as an eternally smiling goddess basking in the sunshine of Elysian fields. Similarly, girls who are led to believe, by reading cheap fiction, that boys thought nothing of committing suicide or changing the course of rivers, like the Iranian lover, would soon learn to look upon their possible husbands as human beings with all the human weaknesses. When a budding Prithwiraj stands stammering before a stern professor, his girl would know that she is not likely to be carried away from her Swayamvara Mandap from the midst of assembled suitors.

The great drawback of co-education lies in the unequal number of boys and girls that attend schools. The girls are so few that they tend to become the centre of attraction. This evil can be remedied only by vigorously encouraging women's education.

If the allegation that students in institutions of co-education, especially in colleges, are more interested in one another than in their studies, is true, we should feel rather hopeful than dejected. We do not want too much of learning for the generality of our boys and girls. At present, they cram so many abstract things that when they come out of the colleges they are fit for nothing but arguing about the theory of relativity or the nature of the atom. Those who have a special aptitude for abstract studies would take to them in spite of the presence of the members of the opposite sex, and the others would naturally manage to fail and get back to practical politics. And if they have failed to acquire knowledge about the attributes of the soul and the size of the electron, they will have gained much knowledge about things which make life worth living. In short, if co-education is a hindrance to higher education, so much the worse for higher education.

I know there is a moral objection to co-education. In a debate I heard on the subject, one of the speakers, a small oldish man with a receding forehead and a voice out of all proportion to his size, cried that men and women were like gunpowder and fire which, if brought together, would be dangerous. The simile went home and preacher after preacher came forward to dilate upon this gunpowder theory. The audience, too, were entering the spirit of the thing. I, however, rose to a point of order and wanted to know whether the theory held good in case of brother and sister, mother and son and father and daughter. Everybody was outraged and I forbear to mention the epithets some adorned me with. All the same, the gunpowder plot was heard no more and people began to talk of something more interesting and less revolting.

And that brings us to the taboo between brother and sister and the power of education in restraining men and women from indulging in premature sexual intercourse. This taboo had its origin in the necessity of keeping boys and girls of the same house apart. Those who believe that God made the brother and sister sexually repugnant to each other would do well to use their intelligence and try to imagine what would be the result if a boy and his sister were separated in early childhood and brought together in youth without knowing the relationship between them. There are communities among whom marriages between brother and sister are permitted and in these communities giving a girl outside one's family is considered a blot on the good name of the family. Queens of Egypt used to marry their brothers and rule with them. This inbreeding, we are told, was productive of a continuous line of geniuses. There is biblical sanction, too, for marrying brothers and sisters. Adam's children married one another.

Again, there is the taboo existing in certain communities regarding marriage between first cousins. Although these communities look upon first cousins as brothers and sisters, there are others, like the Muslims, to whom first cousins are

Emancipation of Women

the legitimate sexual partners. And it remains to be proved that the Muslims are any the worse for it.

Among the Nayars, too, they marry first cousins; but cousins brought up in the same house are looked upon as brothers and sisters and marriage between them taboo. That is, a Nayar cannot marry a daughter of his mother's sister, but he can marry a daughter of his mother's brother, the latter not belonging to his family and not living in the same house; another proof of the fact that the taboo between brother and sister was formulated to keep youngsters of the same house from indulging in premature sex-experience.

We, who have created a brother and sister and first cousins taboo, need not despair of keeping young men and women within reasonable limits by education.

If I advocate mixed bathing and dancing for bringing men and women together, to give them opportunities for forming matrimonial alliances, I would immediately be put down as a despicable imitator of cheap Westernism. But from the following passage in the *Mahabharata*, which describes a waterside picnic in detail, it will be found that love of life and rhythm are not the monopoly of people that side of Constantinople.

"Inflamed by plentiful libations of Kadamba liquor, Balarama the majestic danced in joy with his wife, the daughter of Revata, sweetly beating regular time with his hands. Beholding this the damsels were delighted. The wise and noble Krishna, to enhance the enjoyment of Bala, commenced to dance with his wife Satyabhama. The mighty hero Partha, who had come to this seaside picnic with great delight joined Krishna with the slender and lovely Subhadra. The wise Gada, Sarana, Pradyamana, Samba, Satyaka, and others of the heroic race danced with joy. Through the god-like glory of the heroic and most ardent dancers of the Yadu race, the creation smiled in joy and all the sins of the princes were subdued."

Rishies, too, were not as serious-minded as we take them to be. For "the Brahmarshi Narada, the revered of the gods, came to the scene for the gratification of Madhu Sudana and in the midst of the noble Yadavas, began to dance with his matted locks all dishevelled. He became the central figure in the scene and danced with many a gesticulation and contortion of his body, laughing at Satyabhama and Kesava, at Partha and Subhadra, at Balarama and the worthy daughter of the King of Revata. By mimicking the actions of some, the smile of others, the demeanour of a third sect, and by similar other means, he set all a-laughing who had hitherto preserved their gravity."*

After the dance was over, "Krishna took by hand the venerable sage Narada of imperturbable mind and coming to the sea water along with his wife Satyabhama, Arjuna and others addressed Satyaki with a smile, saying, 'Let us enter the delightful water with the ladies in two parties.' "

Here follows an orgy of mixed bathing, the two parties, one headed by Krishna and the other by Balarama, enjoying a mock battle fought with water. There were hundreds of ladies present and the wit of Narada throws everybody into convulsions of laughter.

The bath over, the party adjourns to the banqueting hall where mutton, buffaloes roasted on spits, haunches of venison cooked in different ways, and shoulders dressed in

* Rajendra Lala Mitra: *Indo-Aryans.*

Emancipation of Women

Ghee are served with Maireya, Asava, Sura, and other exhilarating drinks.

And so we have the sanction of our ancestors for picnicking, dancing, and mixed bathing. There is no harm in letting young men and women take to these with a view to opportunities for knowing their future life-partners at close quarters.

While these positive institutions of free social intercourse between men and women should be actively encouraged, the negative influences that keep men and women apart should receive even greater attention.

The reader must very often have seen the spectacle of young men collecting round ladies' compartments on railway platforms and indulging in mirth-provoking antics to attract the attention of the occupants. They frequent beaches and riversides, too, where European, Anglo-Indian, and such Indian women as have discarded the veil disport themselves in the water, and stand blinking at them like dazed owls. This is an objectionable practice and should strongly be put down. The right way of putting it down is not, however, to post Pathan Chowkidars with big sticks on beaches and riversides to chase away male loafers or by refusing platform tickets to dandies. Nor would a further curtailment of women's freedom bring about the desired result; this would only increase the curiosity of men and women. Moreover, it is stupid not to allow young men to look at girls. The proper cure for this evil is in increasing the freedom of women. Girls should be seen everywhere like boys, in schools, colleges, the street, the highway, the mosque, the temple, and the church. Once girls become common enough, all the glamour of staring at them when stray opportunities arise would naturally vanish. Those who doubt it would be well advised to make a trip to the South, especially Malabar, where women with breasts like the biblical cluster of grapes go about barebodied and unashamed without attracting even the passing attention of men. It is the veil that breeds immoral shame and unnatural curiosity.

It would be beneficial if we abolish the segregation of the sexes in all public places. No railway carriages should be reserved for women. No waiting rooms should be provided specially for women. No seats should be railed off for women at public meetings. No parks should be set apart for Purdah *nishins.*

Some of the above moves might, I know, be objected to on chivalrous grounds. But the word chivalry covers a multitude of sins. Women are mostly persecuted in the name of chivalry. The economic disinheritance of women is defended on chivalrous grounds; it is contended that motherhood is too onerous a duty for women to have any time for money matters and that men, from a sense of chivalry, are looking after the economic interests of women in addition to their own. Even Purdah is defended on chivalrous grounds.

As such, in our attempts to abolish the segregation of the sexes we should not be deterred by any false sense of chivalry.

Parents who fear universal juvenile promiscuity as a result of letting boys and girls move freely in society betray a profound ignorance of the powers of restraint of their sons and daughters. In spite of the fact that Indian girls, married or unmarried, Hindu or Muslim, have plenty of opportunities to indulge in sin with servants and neighbours, do we not find that the vast majority of them have sufficient self-respect and restraint to keep above such licence? Are we

then to understand that if our girls receive better enlightenment, better example in the family and better individuals
than servants to move with, their sinning propensities would
run promiscuous, to the dissolution of society? Freedom of
social intercourse, moreover, does not mean the end of
restraint.

It must be remembered that even to-day our sexual morality
is largely controlled by public opinion and education and
not by law and the policeman. Those individuals who do
not believe in any of the teachings of the current morality,
are forced to abide by the standards of morality around
them if they want to keep their self-respect. A Bernard Shaw
may be furiously opposed to the moral codes of Mrs. Grundy;
but, talking apart, he prefers to move strictly within the
limits of these codes until a new code is established. Nor did
all the poetic genius of Byron and Shelley prove of any avail
against the society whose codes they broke. Even dictators
with absolute powers think twice before openly flouting
conventional morals. When such is the power of public
opinion and environment on the strongest of individuals, we
can gauge their hold on ordinary people.

Education, and education alone, should be our weapon to
combat premature sex-indulgence. True, on some children
our labours might be lost, but excepting these, which should
be considered mentally or physically defective and treated
as such, almost all youngsters are sure to restrain their
impulses within reasonable limits. In fact, boys and girls have
better control over their impulses than their superiors.
Although the adolescent is fascinated by the romance of sex-
experience, this has not yet degenerated into a daily routine
or a physical necessity as is often the case with older men and

women. The young ones who have not tasted forbidden fruit know not what it is.

Free social intercourse would not lead boys and girls to promiscuity but would rather foster better understanding between the sexes and, to a great extent, minimize the evils caused by the attractions of mere superficial beauty. Moving intimately with one another, many a young man and woman would come to know that all that glitters is not gold. Healthy girls with little physical beauty would be found to possess other excellent attractions, whilst a girl or a boy of much physical attraction might turn out to be vain and stupid.

*   *   *   *   *

Love-marriages would necessarily improve the quality of the race. Under present customs any idiot is able to marry, even a very decent girl, if he has a parent or uncle to arrange the match. A desirable husband or wife is a matter of accident and a bad one is to be suffered as a punishment for past sins. Young men and women feel a sort of helplessness in the matter. But in a society where personal selection decides matrimonial alliances, the tendency of all would be to secure good partners, and idiots and imbeciles would have to go without. Personality being the deciding factor, there would be a general tendency to emulate one another in the proper development of one's personality.

Young men and women with freedom of social intercourse are likely to fall in love half a dozen times or more and to repent as many times before they reach marriageable age. But they will have lost nothing by the experience. They will have known by then that, love or no love, marriage or no marriage, men and women remain men and women and it is impossible to unite two souls into one. They will have known that love and marriage have no power of destroying individuality although these might make them take kindly to each other's failings. Then there would be many boys and girls who would have found the right partner and would wait with joy for the age at which their love would be consummated in marriage.

But love with all its advantages is not an unerring guide to marriage. Young men and women are quite likely to enter into matrimonial connexions without knowing themselves and their partners properly and find out afterwards that they have made mistakes. People are likely to develop, after marriage, traits which they were never suspected to possess before. A man, for example, may develop criminal propensities due to changes in his thyroid gland. He might go insane. He might fall in love with another woman and neglect his wife. Marriage, after all, is a human affair and human affairs are neither perfect nor infallible. The wise man, therefore, in all his decisions leaves a margin for mistakes. So does a wise society. Hence, the necessity in a wise Indian society, of

DIVORCE*

If the objection to divorce is founded on the belief that marriages are made by the Almighty, one would like to know what prevents the Almighty from dissolving an ill-contracted union. If the argument is that God in his infinite wisdom cannot make mistakes, the reply is that the street,

* Since this was written, a bill has been introduced in the Central Legislature by Dr. Desh Mukh for permitting divorce among Hindus under certain conditions.

the cremation ground, and the widow bear witness against Him. We have childless marriages, unhappy marriages, and marriages of lepers with excellent women. Cases are on record wherein a woman posing as a man married another woman to get over some exceptional difficulty. If these are not mistakes and if these unions are indissoluble there is no point in human beings claiming the faculty of rational thinking. In fact, it is neither Brahma, Prajapati, nor "Our Father that art in heaven" that makes marriages, but men and women, and very stupid men and women at that.

Time was when men pretended that marriage gave them proprietary rights over women for all eternity. "So strong is the idea of a wife belonging exclusively to her husband that among several people she has to die with him. He may want her in the other world, or, in any case, she shall not be able to become the wife of another." (Westermark.) Sati is an illustration of how strong the idea was among the Hindus. Among Muslims, too, there is a belief that the wives of the Faithful would accompany them to Paradise and minister to them with the houris. Now, a very awkward situation will arise in heaven among communities who look upon polyandry with horror if divorces and remarriages are permitted. This accounts for the religious objection to divorce. But in spite of the Paradise of the Mullahs and theologians, there is a considerable amount of common sense and worldly wisdom in Islam and hence Islamic law permits divorces.

Fanatical insistence on the indissolubility of marriage might at times lead to very awkward situations. If, in a particular community, widow-marriages are permitted and divorce not, a woman might re-marry on the strength of reports of her husband's death which might subsequently prove false. Such cases have happened. A legal situation of this nature arose in Tolstoy's time in Russia and he caught hold of the absurdity of the situation and wrote a tragedy in which the former husband of the woman who ought to have died but did not die was made to commit suicide.

This, no doubt, was an extreme case. But there are many cases, which, while legally not so embarrassing, yet in practical life lead to greater misery. And much of this unnecessary misery can be avoided by making our marriage laws sane.

The chief objections to divorce come from ascetics and from happily married people. We cannot argue with the ascetic about sex, as sex to him is sin and arguments about it a further sin. He is concerned with the hereafter. As regards the happily married, we are more or less on a terrestrial plane. Their objection to divorce is that since their own married life is happy, other people are themselves responsible for their married misery. Healthy individuals, on the same principle, can object to hospitals. It is true that over-eating, over-indulgence in sex, Yogic contemplation, writing bad books of the type turned out by recluses fed on spirituality, and a thousand other things which reasonable people ought to refrain from, are responsible for making many men and women sick. All the same, we do not leave these misguided people to die without medical aid. Similarly, ill-contracted unions may be the outcome of folly on the part of the contracting parties; but it is inhuman to insist on their living in their folly once they want to escape from it. Moreover, accidents play a considerable part in the health of people as well as in the happiness of married life. Men and women who have their bones broken in an earthquake cannot be

Women and Marriage in India

denied medical aid on the ground that they ought to have lived in 'quake-proof buildings. The accidents of married life are of a more complicated nature inasmuch as two people become sufferers for the folly or misdeeds of one. A man might murder his friend because of an unfounded suspicion, fail in an attempt on the life of his wife and be transported for life to Andamans; and it is scarcely fair to insist on his wife remaining celibate for life in memory of his misdeeds.

Swami Dayanand finds a solution for exceptional circumstances in an extensive application of Niyoga. But Niyoga takes into account only the necessity for procreation and raising up seed for a dead, impotent or absent man by a relative or friend. While procreation, no doubt, is the primary object of marriage, companionship, and mutual love are also necessary for the happiness of parents and children. The child requires a father as well as a mother for its proper and balanced development, and it is cruel to deprive a child of the love of a father when we can help it. Dayanand's solution is founded on the infallibility of the Vedas and on the fear of the hell called Put and not on sound human instincts. The days of raising up seed to a dead man by canvassing the services of a living friend are gone for good. If the social arrangements of Vedic India had need of Niyoga, New India has no need of it. Enlightened Indians do not believe in the hell called Put. And decency demands that if any impotent man believes in it and cannot redeem himself by begetting a son, he must face Put as best as he can without creating embarrassing situations for his friends and wife. The rational thing to do in such circumstances would be to grant a divorce and give the woman a chance to fulfil her maternal mission by marrying some man capable of raising offspring. Let us once and for all

Emancipation of Women

rid ourselves of our Vedic and Puranic superstition and behave like human beings.

The fear that divorces would lead to the breaking up of the home, due to men and women marrying and divorcing twice a week, is expressed only by people whose opinion of themselves and their fellow-beings is that they are worse than beasts. Even among beasts, we find that conjugal fidelity exists to a remarkable degree. There are lovers among animals who pine away when separated from mates. Some birds are strictly monogamous and most birds are faithful for seasons. Is it then probable that the vast majority of Hindus would take to promiscuity the moment divorces are permitted by Hindu law? If the answer is in the affirmative, I would like to know what it is that stops a Hindu at present from becoming as promiscuous as he cares to be. Neither the law nor the policeman can stop him from taking the broad road that leads to the brothel. Not only can they not stop him, but they actively assist him on his way to the promiscuous woman. The State gets a good income from the brothels and the police gangs of the locality are under the pay of prostitutes, procurers, and keepers of houses of ill-fame. Any policeman in the street can tell an inquirer where to find the most desirable or undesirable public woman. Yet, with all the facilities the State and an obliging police force afford, do not most men keep to their wives and children? And this in spite of the fact that their wives and children are ugly and tiresome. Are we then to understand that if we raise the quality of our women and children and eliminate tyranny and discord from home-life by means of divorce, our men and women would become less home-loving than they are already?

Women and Marriage in India

The trouble about moralists is that they know too much of logic and very little of human nature. If divorces are made possible they do not find any reason why they should not become general. They forget that there are sound human sympathies that stand in the way of frivolous divorces. Moreover, marriage and social life are something of an interlocking arrangement, and even with the most liberal divorce laws in the world there would be plenty of restraining influences in the society which would make frivolous divorce difficult for respectable people.

The existence of a particular piece of legislation does not mean that it should be taken full advantage of by all. Things that are lawful are not always expedient. There is the law, for example, of slander, which gives a person the right to sue another who calls him a fool or a knave. Yet, it is doubtful if there is a single person alive who hasn't decried his friends and enemies, and among the gay and young, the occasions when one person calls another names can be counted by the dozen a day, and if all this breach of public peace were to lead to court cases, there would not be magistrates enough in the whole of India to try the cases that occur in a single city. About assaults, too, only an insignificant percentage reach the courts. All the same, the laws regarding damages and assaults are quite sane and we cannot do without them. Similarly, we will have to permit divorces in the hope that the law will be made use of only in those cases wherein the parties find it quite impossible to live together. And we have reason to believe that most married couples would stay together in spite of the most liberal laws regarding divorce. Even among friends of the same sex we find constancy lasting for life, although no legal and domestic obligations are involved. People who have real friends know the sorrows of the spirit when estrangements or separations occur. If mere friendship has such a hold on the mind, how much should love and the intimacy of sexual relationship keep men and women together? Is it likely that people who have loved from their youth onwards, eaten from the same dish and shared the same bed, would run to the divorce court if one fine morning the husband found the breakfast ill-cooked and told his wife as much?

Then there is the child. Children are the connecting link between parents and where children are loved divorces would be scarce. The children help the parents to keep together and tolerate many a failing. Even when the fire of young love has died, the sublime flame of old love would still linger in the heart of the parents, and the child is a living argument in favour of liberal divorce laws. All vital impulses, as Ellen Key aptly points out, are conservative and that is what makes the social reformer so bold.

Yet we would be making a grave error if we suppose that all people would be scrupulous in taking advantage of divorce laws. In a community wherein men and women can be divorced freely, there would be pleasure-hunters who would make sport of love and marriage. But are there not pleasure-hunters in every society? Has all our matrimonial tyranny purged society of the prostitute and her consort? Is there not many a man among us who brings the shameless woman to his home, asks his wife to serve her and goes to bed with her, leaving his wedded wife to loneliness and tears? Do not men buy diseases in the bazaar and transmit them to their wives? Are there not debauchees among us who introduce drunkenness and dissoluteness to innocent women? All these people we have in our society and the conditions that obtain to-day are very dangerous for decent women and children. If free divorces are permitted people of stable temperament, who might have, by mistake, allied themselves to the wrong people, would rectify their error and, having learnt by experience, would enter into better matrimonial contacts. And soon, either the pleasure-hunter would better his ways or drop into society fit for him.

We hear much of the modern American miss who makes extensive use of the divorce laws of her country. But we hear very little about the thousands of happy American homes held together by mutual love in spite of easy divorce, because these have no news-value. Moreover, actors and actresses are out to get publicity and it is unfair to judge Americans by the standard of morality that obtains in Hollywood.

Divorce is the test of marriage. Marriages held together with the full consciousness of free divorce are the only ones worth having. All the rest are tyranny. The fear of divorce is the beginning of matrimonial wisdom.

A word about conditional divorces. Adultery and bodily violence when established in a court of law are, in certain countries, considered to be valid reasons for a divorce. The ridiculousness of these conditional divorces is delightfully satirized by Bernard Shaw in his play *Getting Married*. In this comedy, a married girl finds herself in love with another man. The husband, who loves his wife dearly, not in the romantic sense but according to the dictates of common sense, agrees to dissolve the marriage so that the girl may marry the man she loves and be happy with him. But legally, a divorce cannot be granted without adultery or wife-beating.

Emancipation of Women

The husband, taking no risks, decides to do both. And to have the necessary witnesses handy, he beats his wife in the presence of his gardener and makes a public exhibition of himself in the company of a woman well-known for her lack of principle.

When we read of an American woman divorcing her husband on account of the "mental anguish" caused by his snoring, we are not to understand that these gentle bedroom melodies of an American male are in any way more anguishing to his wife than the passage of tramcars down the street, but that what the woman is after is a divorce and she is merely looking for the necessary legal excuses. When two people wish to separate, we can rest assured they will create conditions of separation fast enough. Conditional divorce is an absurdity. The only condition should be the desire of one or both parties to part. If one party seeks a divorce and the other doesn't, it looks unfair to force a divorce on the unwilling party. Painful as the affair is, it cannot be helped. A young man may love a girl to the point of distraction but unless the girl reciprocates his love nobody has the right to force her to marry him. Similarly, we cannot force a person to stick to another when he or she resents it.

Then there is the question of the care and maintenance of the children of divorced parents. Although children might keep many parents together even when a hundred abuses cry for a divorce, it cannot be overlooked that there will be cases wherein parents with children would ask for divorce. At present, the right of the State over the child is but nominal and the child is more or less the property of the parents. For the State to take over the child is neither desirable nor practicable for a long time to come. Nowhere, except in a

Women and Marriage in India

family, can a child get that affection and warmth of feeling which only a parent can give. Stepmothers and stepfathers, although they are by no means the monsters they are generally depicted to be, come very short of real parents. Under these circumstances, where do the children of a divorced couple go?

Other things being equal, mother-right should be given preference over father-right. It is the mother who carried the child nine months in her womb and her claims for guardianship come first. Only if she be willing to forgo her claims should the child be given to its father. And, unless the State has reason to believe that a mother is likely to abuse her trust and bring up the child in a way injurious to society, it may not deprive her of her child.

As compared with mothers, fathers are generally indifferent to children. They do not know children, they expect them to behave like adults, even beat them when they behave like children and very often show a degree of indifference. With all this, however, it is but just that a father should do something for the maintenance and protection of the child he has created. Divorce should not give him license to waste his money in taverns and brothels when it could be utilized for its maintenance. And so, even when the child is retained by its mother, its father should be compelled to contribute substantially. The amount of money that should be paid must be in direct proportion to the number of children, taking into consideration the man's earnings. This arrangement would put an effective stop to irresponsible parenthood and to frivolous divorces. A man with, say, ten children and a salary of Rs. 100 a month will have, when divorced, to forgo most of his pay for the sake of his children leaving him to live a hand-to-mouth existence. And since the fear of starvation is the beginning of wisdom, men and women would learn to be responsible beings in parenthood and divorce.

In a society of free divorce, there might even be parents both of whom disclaim the children. Such cases, supposing they occur, should be treated as accidents. Even now we have children whose parents die leaving them destitute. We have exposed babes, too, who remain unclaimed. Divorced parents, if they are wage earners, would be compelled to pay for the maintenance of their children and they will be brought up in an orphanage.

When all is said, the balance is struck in favour of free divorce. Imbeciles, idiots, criminals, and lepers may rightly object to liberal divorce laws as they may not be able to keep the partners they secured by chance or cunning. But humanity as a whole is more important than the few defectives, and it is better that these should go without partners than that the whole community be contaminated by them.

If marriages and divorces are left completely to the will of individuals, where does the necessity for legislation come? Why not mate and separate as we like and abolish the institution of marriage altogether and live in what is called free love?

The objection to this sexual anarchy, again, is in respect of the child. So long as the guardianship of the child rests with the parents and not with the State, some sort of State-control in the matter of reproduction and rearing of children is necessary as every child is a potential citizen. State recognition of marriage is necessary to establish the fatherhood of children when the question of maintenance of children is raised. The child is the father of the marriage and were it not for the question of rearing, there would have been no

Women and Marriage in India

marriage, no family, and no home. And so long as men and women have instincts of protection and affection towards their offspring, it is good that marriage and family life continue. The home can be made a good thing, although some modern thinkers have lost hope and advocate the destruction of marriage and the dissolution of the family. They are the impatient revolutionaries of a reforming era, but they are a force to be reckoned with and the fanaticism of conventional moralists is likely to strengthen their hands.

In the present state of Indian society, the most liberal divorce laws would merely remain in the Statute Book without affecting society in any way. This is evident from the fact that among Muslims, to whom divorce is almost as easy as to Americans, there are very few actual cases. This is not because Muslim marriages are ideal but because of the enormous disabilities of Muslim women. A woman who is illiterate and does not know what her rights are and who is not allowed to move about without her husband's permission is not likely to take the initiative and go to a law-court for divorce. Again, women are so abjectly dependent upon their husbands that they would rather put up with any amount of tyranny than precipitate a divorce and make their children and themselves destitute. A Muslim woman would rather let her husband marry three more women and be a fourth-rate wife to him than assume the condition of an unowned woman. In these circumstances, any liberality in the matter of divorce would merely widen the scope of the heartless and increase the misery of women and children. It is therefore imperative that, before making divorces free and easy, we must free woman from the tyranny of man for ever. And this leads us to the crux of the problem; namely,

Emancipation of Women

The first step in the direction of the economic emancipation of women should be taken by amending the present laws of inheritance, so that daughters may inherit parental wealth equally with sons. Woman being a greater asset to the race than man, and likely to suffer more by destitution and want, chivalry demands that she should be better provided for economically than man. But chivalry in India is confined to poetry and fiction, and we can hardly expect men to treat women with preference. But democracy and decency demand that women should not be treated as inferiors in the matter of inherited wealth.

The objection to this, again, is found in Manu. According to his authority, a wife cannot own wealth. Moralists, too, there are who tell us that women are incapable of handling money. But experience belies Manu and the moralist. Wherever women have had freedom, they have amply proved that they are fit for economic independence; wherever they have been trusted with financial responsibility, they have borne it with even greater success than men. Elizabeth, Victoria, Nurjehan, and many a Hindu queen are examples of women who have managed men and finance with commendable skill. It cannot be argued that feminine capability is confined to royalty. We come across many a housewife but for whose capability the house would sink to ruin. In the face of this it is childish to argue that women should not be allowed to possess wealth equally with men.

Even where the present laws are favourable to women in the matter of inheritance, most women are unable to take advantage of them, because of their ignorance of their privileges and their inability to secure sympathy and support. Society looks down upon a woman who moves the law against those of her male relatives who profit by her ignorance. The formation of a society of women actively to hunt out oppression and secure legal redress for women and children is urgently necessary in India. A woman who goes to court against her husband or relatives should not be looked upon as shameless but rather as a martyr or a heroine. Just as breaches of Sarda Act are brought to light and culprits prosecuted by members of Indian Women's Conference Association, public-spirited bodies should be formed to exploit the positive side of the law so that women may benefit fully from their privileges, small as they are. There are innumerable cases of brothers, husbands, and uncles who prey upon the wealth of their female wards and leave them helpless and miserable, and these should be mercilessly exposed so that women may become aware of their rights without which the most liberal laws regarding inheritance are not likely to produce any remarkable effect.

Together with the change in the law of inheritance, women should be given equal opportunity with men to acquire wealth. This, to the superficial observer, might look like a plea for creating employment for women. At a time when we are unable to find employment even for the few of our educated young men, the demand for employment for our millions of adult females will be dismissed as ridiculous. But there is no necessity for us to create employment for women, as almost all of them excepting the inmates of harems are in the enjoyment of work. Our problem is to find not work for them but pay for their work.

The problem of economic independence for women

Emancipation of Women

scarcely exists among the working classes, whether they be toilers in the fields or industrial workers. Although the wages paid to women workers are generally lower than those paid to men, for all practical purposes working-class women are more or less independent economically. The wife-beating propensities of the labourer may be attributed to the muscular superiority of the male rather than to his economic superiority.

Among the educated rich, too, women are socially and economically independent. Of course the old-fashioned rich still shut their women up in the harem, but these are numerically negligible and are fast dying out. That leaves us once again with the miserable middle class.

For the middle class of the countryside and small town we can do very little at present. They are mostly peasants and petty shopkeepers and it will take long time before the authority of the State reaches their domestic life. For the middle classes of the cities, however, we can do something. They are mostly employees in government service or in the service of well-known firms. That makes it easy to deal with them.

If we rid ourselves of the idea that a married woman's domestic service is not worth paying for, we should find very little difficulty in effecting the economic emancipation of middle-class women in the cities. These women are doing very essential work and there is no reason why they should not be paid for it. When a man pays his servant to cook bad meals, mismanage his domestic affairs, and steal his money, why should he not pay for the services of his wife, who is more honest and efficient than a servant? Why should marriage be used as an institution which can command

Women and Marriage in India

feminine slave labour? When a woman does work worthy of wages why should she be compelled to beg for her necessities, even if it be from her husband? Has she not every right to demand of him a certain remuneration for her services?

If women were paid for domestic services, it will be argued, the arrangement would reduce the sacred ties of matrimony to a servant-master relation. It will, if the wife receives her pay from her husband. But even if this were the case, it would be a definite improvement on present relations which are of a slave-master kind. But there is a grave objection to leaving husbands to pay their wives. The objection is that, left to themselves, they wouldn't do it. Even if the State demands receipts, the husbands could produce them without having paid a single pie to their wives.

Therefore, to make the law effective and women independent, something more practical should be done. A good beginning can be made by passing a law by which half or a definite portion of the salary of an employee be paid to his wife. She should receive it direct from the office of the employee and no letter of authority should be entertained. The lady should come in person, sign for her pay, and take it home. Adopting this system for all employees in government service would revolutionize the position of Indian women in a single year to an extent very little appreciated. In addition to effecting the economic independence of thousands of women, it would give women an opportunity for social intercourse as would nothing else.

If the prejudice against women's independence be overcome, middle-class women would find no difficulty in taking to profitable professional work too. Apart from the learned

154

Emancipation of Women

professions like law and medicine, women can engage themselves in a number of independent tasks which would bring them profit and happiness. Her Highness, the Maharanee of Baroda, in her useful work, *Position of Women in Indian Life*, gives an exhaustive list of such tasks. Horticulture, dairy-farming, cericulture, landscape-painting, landscape-gardening, furniture designing, art-dealing, baking, and weaving are some of them.

In all departments of State service women can be employed in large numbers, and professions peculiarly suited to their genius should be reserved. The primary education of children is essentially woman's province and no man should be allowed to teach in primary classes. Nursing and midwifery go unquestionably to women. Women can be employed in railways as ticket collectors, checking staff, and booking clerks to the greater comfort of passengers; their dealings with the public are likely to be less provocative, for to-day much of the time of legislatures is wasted by members attacking railway servants who did not reserve lower berths and coupé compartments for them. A considerable portion of the daily papers is also allotted to the airing of grievances against railway staffs. The liberal appointment of women in checking and information departments would reduce these complaints to a minimum. In spite of all that is said about talkative women and nagging wives, none would deny that women are more courteous and civil to customers than men.

Taking women in large numbers into State employment might lead to denying government jobs to many men. It is doubtful if this would be a mistaken policy. By hankering after clerking and teaching young men of India are losing much of their practical ability. Their ambitions should be diverted from the economic security of small government jobs to success in less certain, adventurous enterprises. Once they are made to understand that government jobs are not worth so much seeking they would look for something better, provided we discourage the present tendency of disappointed young men to take to religious indolence. If they had any energy they would take to independent professions, commerce, insurance agency, or piracy, and all of these, with the exception of the last, are likely to yield splendid results after the humiliations of the initial stages are overcome. Whether they make good in these enterprises or not, under no circumstances should they be allowed to stand in the way of women and their living. Although our ultimate ideal is the equality of the sexes to the extent Nature would permit, as a transitional measure women may be given preference over men in the matter of government employment so as to put them on a sound economic footing.

It is also possible to employ women in large numbers without dismissing men, if we would allow ourselves a little humanity in our search after profit. Most of the employees in the factories and the railways are overworked. In the railways particularly, the thousands of employees that run the system daily do eight hours duty and more. Where work is done day and night, the twenty-four hours are divided into three shifts of eight hours each. And this eight hours' night duty is so injurious to the sight and general health of the employees that the number of those who fail in vision test and medical examination before reaching superannuation is considerable. Humanity requires that the daily duty of railway employees be cut down to six hours. This would raise the necessary number of employees in the ratio of three to four.

Most of our hospitals, too, are under-staffed. In many hospitals, there are nurses who perform twelve hours night duty. This is cruel not only to the nurses but to the patients as well. It is not likely that a girl walking about for twelve hours among sick men and women would be as kind to patients as she ought to be. The night duty of nurses should be halved and double the present number should be taken on.

But who would pay this increased army of workers? That truly is a problem. Dismissing the Shavian solution of work for all and equality of pay as too extreme for the present conditions in India, we are left with two alternatives. One is to ask the Finance Member to pay up; the other is to effect an all-round reduction in salaries proportionate to the increase in employees. Although the former solution is preferable, the latter is more practicable. Adopting the latter solution, of course, would lead to low start in salaries and a young man will have to wait for a long time to marry, especially if he is to marry a girl without employment. But it might be a social improvement thus to raise the marriage age by economic necessity.

With an increase in the number of independent women, there would be families of two earning persons who will be held together by mutual love without financial motives. These families would naturally be our ideal. The couple would work in their respective offices among their co-workers and the family would be the quiet abode of love, where they spend their leisure and the night in the enjoyment of each other's company. When a child is born, the parents would find an additional joy in the home, and family life

Women and Marriage in India

would become as perfect as is possible in a world of imperfections. People in a permanent mood of protest will find in
the child an argument against this sort of family. If both the
parents go to their offices, they will say, there would be
nobody to look after the child, which might climb over the
balcony of the flat into the street. But two earning people can
easily afford at least one reliable servant to whom the care
of the child can be entrusted in the absence of its parents.
Those who contend that children looked after by servants
would be spoilt physically and morally and that a mother
alone can look after a child for twenty-four hours of a
day need not be taken seriously. Many Englishmen, who in
childhood, are bottle-fed and reared by nurses, Ayahas and
governesses, to-day rule over Indians who are breast-fed
and brought up under the continual vigilance of their
mothers. Too much mothering is as injurious to children
as over-feeding. We have nothing to fear if a child is left
with proper trained servants for a few hours a day when its
parents are working elsewhere.

The prosperity and well-being of India would be directly
proportionate to the number of such families of independent
men and women held together by mutual love and understanding. In such a family there would be no place for
suspicion, fear, bullying, nagging, keeping the Zenana out
of reach of men's eyes and all the thousand and one imbe-
cilities that make the present middle-class home in India a
pocket edition of Pandemonium.

But for the maintenance of such families it is not only
necessary to take women in large numbers into public service,
but also to remove the senseless prejudices obtaining at
present among employers against marriage and motherhood.

Emancipation of Women

While the value of virgins in the matrimonial market can be understood, it is not known why employers of feminine labour and the State should prefer them. In all the professions peculiarly suited to women, such as teaching, nursing, and midwifery mothers are likely to turn out better work than virgins and bachelor-girls. A woman who has children of her own would be a much more understanding and sympathetic teacher of children than one who has none; a woman who has experienced the travail of childbirth herself would be a better midwife than one who has no such experience; and, a woman who has a husband, a child, and a home to care for would take better interest in the work which supports her than a girl with a powdered nose and painted lips whose interest in the office lies more in flirting with her employer than in her legitimate work. All told, mothers and married women are more responsible and efficient workers than unmarried girls.

Again, humanity requires that working women should not be treated as though they have no sex or maternal instincts. Thwarting of instincts make men and women cruel, unsocial, and even anti-social. The cruelty of some schoolmistresses towards children can be attributed to this. If nurses in our hospitals are allowed to marry the condition of patients can be much improved. Herding the girls in barracks attached to hospitals is responsible for much of their callousness. If they are allowed to marry and settle down and attend to their work like other people, not only would the condition of patients be improved, but the prowling of men about hospital quarters and the undesirable institution of "taking the girls out" would also disappear.

The appointment of married women would necessarily

entail shorter working hours and more liberal leave rules. In the months of pregnancy and lactation every woman is entitled to privilege leave. These liberal leave rules would again mean more employment. There is no cause for alarm in this; our problem to-day is one of unemployment, and not of over-employment. If there is not as much profit as we would wish to have, let us share what we have. And, since all our men and women are managing to live somehow or other at present (most of the unemployed live in dependence upon their relatives) it is foolish to argue that if we give the idlers work and share our profits with them society would degenerate. If anything at all would be in danger it would be the abnormal profit of a few. And humanity, being greater than a few heartless individuals, it would be, on the whole, a good thing that their profits are restricted.

The solution of our city brothels, too, lies in attracting more women to the city by giving them honourable means of livelihood. The present proportion of men to women in every Indian city is approximately two to one. Making allowance for polygynists and widows, more than half the men of our cities are condemned to barrack-life. What are they to do? Moralists would advise them to practise continence and would preach its great spiritual advantages. The State knows better. It knows that if celibacy is forced upon half the male population of a city, the result would be an uncontrollable spread of vice, violence, and crime. It is doubtful whether in such a society the wives and daughters of moralists would remain in peace with their husbands and fathers. The State, therefore, relieves the situation by legalizing brothels. This, no doubt, is one way of solving the problem. But condemning a small group of helpless, wretched

women to the instinct of more than half of the male population of a large city is far from a human solution. It is a Satanic
solution. It would be a thousand times more human and
moral if every married man in the city allowed a friend or
two to make love to his wife. The best solution, however,
would be to equalize the numerical disparity of the sexes.
Otherwise all the work of our vigilance societies is doomed
to fail. There is no point in seeking to suppress symptoms
while leaving the cause to pursue its own way.

Apart from giving all possible encouragement to women
to take to profitable work, modern thought is tending to
think of motherhood itself as work worthy of payment.
This tendency is more in evidence among people of the
West where a decreasing birth-rate alarms dictators and
politicians who are competing with one another in raising
human crops for the sickle of the next war. In India, we have
no such fears. War or no war, we have always enough men
and to spare and our mothers can be counted in crores. If
the State is going to take all these swarms of mothers seriously
and pay them on the broad principle that motherhood is
work worthy of payment, there would be very little left in
the treasury to keep the State going.

Yet a desirable reform can be introduced by the State
paying model mothers. Girls may be selected, having due
regard to their physical and mental fitness, given training
in the duties of motherhood, with diplomas for worthy
candidates. Such women may be held up as examples to others
and they may be paid so much per child to a maximum of
say three or four children. If the competition for model
motherhood becomes too great for the State to make payment,
this obligation may be abolished; by that time enough women

Women and Marriage in India

will have realized that ideal motherhood is an end in itself whether paid by the State or not.

*   *   *   *   *

What Indian society would be like if women were emancipated need not remain to us a matter of speculation and argument. We have in Russia a sister country that has emancipated its women and has given them equal rights with men in all spheres of public and private life. But Indian patriots would object to any comparison between the two countries on the ground that India and Russia are poles apart geographically and culturally. Hence it is necessary to prove to them first that India and Russia have not only many things in common, but that the condition of Czarist Russia was strikingly similar to that of present-day India. The ignorance of the masses, the tyranny of bureaucrat and priest, and the wretchedness and superstitions of the peasantry were all familiar features of Czarist Russia; India has exactly the same problems to solve to-day. The people of pre-revolutionary Russia were as "spiritually-minded" as Indians and there were more icons in Russia than there are idols in India. The whole country was infested with wandering mendicants who, as in India, bullied and preyed upon the poor. The poverty of the average Russian was as acute as that of the Indian to-day; and as people in India explain away their iniquities by the law of Karma, the Russian clergy explained away the misery of the poor as an inexorable law of God, for, without the poor, the pious could not practise the virtue of charity.

The position of women under the Czars was in no way better than is that of Indian women. Russia, too, had her

Emancipation of Women

Manu and Kautilya. The following extract from the *Domostroy*, the Russian moral code of the sixteenth century, is worth noting:

"If a wife refuses to obey and pays no attention to what her husband tells her, it is advisable to beat her with a whip according to the measure of her guilt; but not in the presence of others, rather alone. And do not strike her straight in the face or on the ear; also be careful how you strike her with your fist in the region of the heart and do not use a rod of wood or iron." This moderation is recommended because, "he who allows himself to be carried away to such actions by anger may have much unpleasantness, if, for example, she loses her hearing or goes blind or breaks a bone in her head or foot or elsewhere. Keep to the whip and choose carefully where to strike; the whip is painful and effective; detenent and salutary.

"But if her fault is very serious, the matter not so simple, her disobedience beyond all bound, then strip off her shift, seize her hands and give her a sound beating—nicely and courteously so as to eschew all anger."*

A Russian proverb tells us that "a hen is not a bird nor a woman a human being." The following description of women's lot in old Russia is typical of the lot of Indian women:

> Three hideous portions to woman Fate gave:
> The one: to a slave to be mated;
> The second: the mother to be a slave;
> The third; to a slave subjugated;
> And each of these burdens have heavily lain
> On women of Russia's domain.

* *Woman in Soviet Russia*: Fannina Halle.

163

Women and Marriage in India

And these were the women who took such an outstanding part in the revolutionary movement in Russia which brought into being the new Russian society. That centuries of oppression of women in India have not sapped their vitality is amply proved by the active part they have played in the recent political movement of our country.

Now we shall have a look at the new society of Russia and see what emancipated womanhood is doing. We can quite well be interested in this new Russian society without having to believe in the necessity of shooting Englishmen and Marwari mill-owners. What Russia has achieved by blood, India may achieve without bloodshed. It might take a longer time, perhaps, but it is worth while waiting.

There are people in India who, after reading all the filth that is circulated about Russia, seem convinced that thousands of Russian revolutionaries (most of whom in affluent circumstances) courted jail, exile, and death just to spite God and damn themselves. Russia, no doubt, in her struggle for freedom made many mistakes and shed much blood without necessity. But it is unfair to judge Russians by their failings alone. During the social cataclysm that followed the revolution, there was anarchy in sexual relations as in everything else. The insecurity of life and property produced by the wars and famine, and the intoxication of sudden freedom from restrictions, made people adopt a fatalistic attitude towards life, and a philosophy of futility made its appearance, reducing sexual relationships to an unimportant factor comparable to "drinking a glass of water." Love was despised as a *petit-bourgeois* vice, and in the hysterical excitements of the times people practised even more than what they preached. This none can deny. But it was no more the result of women's

Emancipation of Women

emancipation than the Bihar earthquake of Congress propaganda. If you try to imagine what would happen in India if all the machinery of established government disappeared overnight with a handful of Congressmen left to restore order, you have some idea of what happened in Russia in this period. And to this add the fact that the Bolsheviks had to fight the armies of the capitalistic countries as well as their internal enemies. It was very long before an efficient government was able to restore order and bring social life to stability.

But Communism has come to stay in Russia and the new society is rapidly settling down. Russian women have now complete equality with men in all walks of life, not excluding in some respects the army and the navy, and neither sex is any the worse for it.

In Russia, when a man and a woman live together so as to beget children and found a family, it is recognized as marriage. Registration is not essential for recognition, although it is widely encouraged if only to settle paternity in case of dispute. But the fact of cohabitation, when proved and witnessed, is enough to give the aggrieved party all the privileges of registration.

Divorces are easy and free—or were so until recently—and the keeping of the matrimonial obligations are largely left to the good sense of the individuals concerned. The result of this arrangement is an increased sense of self-respect among men and women. A man who shirks the elementary responsibility of supporting his children, the robust Russian woman, economically independent herself, dismisses as a man unworthy of her worry. This attitude has created a healthy sense of honour and responsibility among men, and

Women and Marriage in India

those who desert their wives and children are despised as possessing *petit bourgeois* minds. The Bolshevik outlook on sex is almost Puritanic and one who is given too much to sexual pleasures stands in danger of losing membership of the party.

In proportion to the freedom allowed in the matter of marriage and divorce is the stringency of laws against prostitution. Considering the equality of the sexes in numbers, the elimination of merchants and princes who keep harems and mistresses, the facilities afforded to men and women alike for earning an honourable living, the Communists find no reason why people should open shops for the sale of human flesh. Procurers, and those who encourage their dependents to prostitute themselves, are severely punished and their property confiscated. There are homes for women who have gone astray, where they are taught trades in healthy surroundings and are educated in a respect for the human body.

There is a special Government department in Russia for combating prostitution and every care is taken to see that young girls without guardians are not induced into a life of shame. Such girls are given preference while recruiting employees and officials have special instructions to see that in retrenchment schemes they are treated with special consideration. There is wide propaganda against prostitution and posters are exhibited in public places denouncing it. There is strict police supervision in all places likely to attract unprincipled men and women. Special care is taken to see that the war against prostitution does not degenerate into a war against prostitutes. The Communists believe that women are generally driven to vice by poverty, loneliness, or a love of

Emancipation of Women

excitement caused by ignorance, incomplete education, or mental deficiency. They search for the root of the evil—unlike our own vigilance workers, who recite in their annual report all the good works they have done, send it to Press, and then go to sleep until the time comes for the next report. Abortions are discouraged in Russia as unhealthy and immoral; but in proved cases, where a woman, due to poverty, ill-health, or some such sound reason, cannot afford to bring forth the expected child, abortion is permitted provided a certificate from a competent authority, appointed by the State, is produced. Abortion is not practised by necromancers, witches, or quacks as is the case in India, but by specialists in government hospitals. This Bolshevik honesty in the matter of abortion has revolted all the hypocritical nations of the world, and wild stories are circulated of Soviet immorality.

With all that is said in favour of the new Russian society, none need run away with the idea that the sexual relationship in Russia is blissful and perfect. While it is undoubtedly more civilized and humane than in most other countries, Russians, it must be remembered, whatever their form of government, are human beings with all their failings and weaknesses. Desertions, divorces, and seductions still abound in Russia and are likely to continue for a long time. In cases of divorce and desertion, especially after birth of children, women have a right to sue for the maintenance of their children and they are not deterred by public opinion in their attempts at moving the law against their husbands. In the case of casual connexions leading to pregnancy, the woman has a right to claim maintenance, and there has been many a case recorded wherein a woman had several lovers at the same time, the paternity of the child could not be fixed, and several lovers asked to contribute towards the maintenance of a single child. Such cases are exceptional and should not be allowed to influence our judgments of Russian society. All told, Russia, which until modern times had been the most backward of all the nations of Europe, has caught up with and even passed the foremost of them within less than two decades.

Those who complain that the Bolsheviks have destroyed the family and have reduced humanity to a farmyard or an ant-hill, would do well to read the following summing up of Russian family life, by Fannina Halle, in her book *Woman in Soviet Russia*:

"Whereas in capitalistic countries ever since the war we have heard only the breakdown of the marriage and the decay of the family, in the land of the Soviets it is at least possible to speak with equal justification of a new form of marriage and family which is taking shape. Only the patriarchal family built upon the economic domination and legally sanctioned authority of the husband is doomed to die out and has already lost all its vitality. And it is pretty clear what the new form of marriage and the family in process of growth will be like. They will be based on the full economic, political, and social equality of the sexes. And whereas in Western Europe the matriarchate has actually been contemplated recently as a way of escape from the crisis in marriage and the family, and signs are already discernible of such a development in America, in the Soviet Union, the country where women have attained a position of unprecedented predominance in which certain individuals have held that conditions are making straight for a gynaecocracy, there is

Emancipation of Women

no indications except the Amazon type and the unmarried motherhood, of the possibility that a new matriarchate might rise. Perhaps, the evolution of the New Woman may be regarded in some respects as a continuation of the pre-Christian development which I tried to trace in the indications contained in the ancient epics and in the lingering echoes of the matriarchate; yet, this continuation does not present itself as a revival of the matriarchal traditions, but as the final abolition of the domination of one sex by the other in all their mutual relations: in love, marriage, and the family."

The observations of Allan Monkhouse, a victim of the notorious Moscow trial, confirm this view. "It is true," he says, "that both marriage and divorce are regarded as matters of proper registration involving the payment of a few shillings and the signing of a form. The time and trouble involved are comparable with that required to renew a driving licence in Great Britain. In claiming divorce it is sufficient for one party only to register the annulment of the marriage. The law makes proper provision for the payment of the alimony to support any children there may have been of the marriage. It is a significant fact that the Russian people as a rule do not avail themselves of the extraordinary freedom of action which the legislation permits. The marriage tie in present-day Russia is reasonably permanent."*

The opinion of Mark Patrick, no friend of the Bolsheviks in any way, is also worth quoting. After recounting all that the Communists have done to destroy the family and marriage, he adds that "the bias of humanity towards more or less permanent monogamy is showing itself very resistent to contrary influence. Western Europe, perhaps, begins to

* *Moscow*, 1911–1933.

question whether any such bias exists. But the trend of events in Russia seems to suggest that not only does it exist but that it is decisive. The figures of divorce—that is to say, the ratio of unions cancelled to those officially registered—was very high in the early days of the revolution. People doubtless felt that a general license was the only thing appropriate to the times. But for the last five years or more, the figures has shown a decline until now, I was informed, it is comparable to some of the United States."*

With all respect to the author, it must however be pointed out that the evident bias of humanity towards monogamy in Russia is rather the direct result of Soviet recognition of the equality of the sexes. Promiscuity not being normal to civilized human beings, in a country where men and women are left to adjust sexual relationship without economic or political influences affecting either side, monogamy is the only institution that can maintain itself.

POLYGYNY AND POLYANDRY

are undemocratic institutions. We all know that polygyny degenerated into gross sexual tyranny in patriarchates where women were treated as a form of property. But most people do not know that polygyny in these societies was tyranny over the majority of men as well.

We do not know sufficient about the ancient matriarchates to form a correct idea of the complications that might have arisen from the practice of polyandry. Perhaps in a thorough-going matriarchate, the queen and the noblewomen might

* Patrick: *Hammer and Sickle.*

have appropriated all the handsome young men of the kingdom to themselves, leaving to the common women the old men and defectives. Contemporary matriarchates are more or less under masculine influence and do not show much tyranny to poor women even where polyandry flourishes. Moreover, women have better feeling towards their fellow-beings than men, and it is probable that even in the most pronounced of polyandrous communities they might not have deprived their sisters of the right to found a home. But among patriarchal communities the case had been different.

History tells us that in all patriarchal societies men with sufficient means always managed to keep a number of women to themselves whether the law permitted it or not. In all Asiatic countries, the law favours polygyny. Although the Prophet's law restricted the number of a man's wives to four at a time, his followers found sufficient authority to keep as many women as their wealth could buy. Christian law enforces strict monogamy. But kings and nobles bought or bullied the keepers of the law and gave free rein to their polygynous tendencies by establishing the institution of mistresshood. There were some Christian kings, no doubt, who had scruples. Henry VIII, we know, went to the extent of beheading his wives when new beauties caught his fancy, so as to keep himself within the monogamic codes of the Church. Our own kings were not Christians and had less exacting consciences; they were content to banish their old wives to a corner of the harem when new wives took their places. There are traditions of divine kings among us who thought nothing of keeping sixteen thousand wives, in addition to a sober eight. These things, however, could be done only by kings and sages and not by ordinary mortals. These in all countries

Women and Marriage in India

and in all times were more or less monogamous. Some were
even forced to lead a life of celibacy due to shortage of women
caused by the noble, the merchant, and the king filling their
harems with most of the good-looking women in the kingdom.
Poor men either went without wives or mated with such
women as those on whom the rich did not consider it worth
their while to waste money. Many a Muslim monarch, we
know, had the right to unveil any woman in the street and
order her to his harem.

Monogamy is not so much a sexual virtue as a democratic
virtue. And it is in the West, like all democratic institutions,
that it took root. Each man or woman has a right to a partner,
and if men with power and wealth go about monopolizing
the best of the other sex, it is far from fair to their less
fortunate brethren.

Women themselves do not actively object to polygyny.
Although a woman would feel elated if she is able to command
the exclusive attention of one man, she would certainly
prefer to be one of his many wives than be the sole mistress
of an imbecile. The same can be said of men, too. A man
would rather be one of half-a-dozen husbands to a beautiful
worthy woman than be the undisputed possessor of a nagging
scarecrow.

It is mostly a question of restricting one's cupidity to the
requirements of society. Most men and women would like
to have all the world at their feet if they could possibly
arrange it. Our sense of justice derives its inspiration from
this human rapacity. Since each one of us wants to be the
master of the whole world, we find it imperative to define
the limits of our ambitions, especially where they come into
conflict with the ambitions of others. The fundamental

Emancipation of Women

rapacity of the human heart is at present most evident in industry and commerce, where our ideas of justice still remain primitive and confused. It may be mentioned that our captains of industry, who defend the rights of unlimited acquisition of wealth as divinely bestowed, would soon learn to adjust themselves to the collective convenience of the community, if we were to pass some extreme law to shoot all who possessed private property beyond a certain maximum. In the absence of such a law, the removal from the Statute Books of some of those clauses which actively assist the exploiter, would lead to a satisfactory apportionment of wealth by the disinherited themselves, standing up for their elementary right of life.

The principle applies in sexual relations also. There are men and women who would like to have all members of the opposite sex to themselves. There have been kings who tried to put this into practice. But with the spread of democratic ideas, a rise in the standard of our sense of justice, and, above all, the gradual emancipation of women, this tendency is giving place to monogamy. Times have so changed that even some of our princes have come to think that to have but one wife is not an infringement of their divine rights. Similarly, the pious man who at present cannot without horror see his wife talking to another man would soon learn to share her charms with a dozen others if, say, the number of women suddenly fell to a sixth of its present size, and the State insisted that a woman, married or unmarried, possessed complete rights over her own body, and that if he did not like the arrangement he was at liberty to do without.

Then there are the women of the brothels to whom men go in the full knowledge that each is but one of the crowd.

Women and Marriage in India

Jealousy is no serious impediment to polygyny or polyandry. As already explained in a former chapter it is not sexual jealousy that makes the laws of adultery so stringent but economic jealousy founded on the fear of culckoldom. Most men are jealous because society wants them to be so. Men who consider their wives as nuisances and do not love them, even at a distance, would murder their wives on suspicion of friendly terms with other men, just because society despises the cuckold. Jealousy arising out of love is not half so bad as this artificial form. In fact, in all communities in which custom permits polygyny and polyandry, the several wives or husbands manage very well together. True there are quarrels and bickerings, but these are bound to arise whereever a number of people move freely or intimately. Coolies working in a gang might cut each other's throats without sexual matters having anything to do with it. A boss in an office might take a flying kick at a clerk even though the latter may not have made love to his lady stenographer. Husbands and wives in monogamic households might quarrel over ornaments, Sarees, potato chips, and over the question of beating children. Similarly, in households where two or more wives or husbands live together, there may be any amount of ill-feeling without sexual jealousy having anything to do with it. In fact, the domestic lives of Mohammed and many other oriental potentates show that polygyny, when handled capably, has its advantages. There is nothing sexually sinful either in polygyny or in polyandry, and it must be remembered that where there is scarcity of men polygyny is the only solution to the sex-problem. Shortage of women being extremely rare, the necessity for polyandry is not likely to arise in any country, even in India where we manage to kill so many women by child-marriage and ill-treatment.

But the question is whether in normal times, under normal conditions, we should permit polygyny and polyandry. The answer is, we should not. Although some extra-matrimonial amusement might, instead of having any demoralizing effect, increase people's zest for life, as far as family arrangements go, all must learn to be content with one partner. With the increasing refinement in individual love and selection, few people would find this arrangement disappointing. All normal people would like to preserve love's secrecy and would instinctively avoid a crowd. A family of three or more is to be discouraged, not because men and women would cut each other's throats from jealousy, but because there will always be a majority and minority question which is fatal to free and happy partnership. A partnership of two is the ideal. Even among people of the same sex the maxim holds good.

The only danger to monogamy is over-attachment. Wise people would do well to note that for the full enjoyment of domestic happiness it is necessary that husband and wife should manage to remain separate for the greater part of the day and often for weeks on end. A man who comes home from office, the football field, or a tour is likely to find his home more comfortable than one who sits at home always dreaming of the great happiness of domestic life. And what applies to man applies with equal force to woman. There are some even who advocate living in separate establishments.

While monogamy would be the general tendency in a society of free men and women there would be some exceptions. We know of cases wherein two friends fall in love with one girl and the girl takes a liking to both; so that where there is no objection on the part of any of the three, there is nothing to prevent the girl marrying one of the men and slipping in the other as a family friend, paying-guest, or other respectable person. There are exceptional men and women who are temperamentally polygamous and choke in a monogamic society; and although the law cannot be altered to suit the convenience of these exceptions, we should not be hard upon them; they should be allowed to adjust themselves as best as they can. A mild social contempt towards them would perhaps be salutary, lest their example be followed by others.

There may be a certain type of woman who may put her appearance in the new society: The woman of the type of Shaw's Lesbia, who would like to rear children without a husband permanently attached to her. While all normal women would like the companionship of a man, there are bound to be some who would use him as a mere instrument in the act of reproduction; they might rear their children without the help of a father. But a family which includes a father and mother is a more balanced one for a child to grow in than one with one parent only.

These are the exceptions that form the bulk of those living on the borderland of society. The vast majority of men and women if made tolerably free would form lasting monogamic connexions under normal conditions. This new family, held together by mutual love alone, would save India and help her to find a place among the progressive nations of the world.

CHAPTER IV

Wanted: New Values

★

THE values that obtain in India at present are mostly medieval, discarded already by most other nations of the world for better ones. Everywhere man is liberating himself from the thraldom of traditions and is beginning to think that much of the poverty, misery, and wretchedness which were suffered as inevitable and were attributed to Destiny, God, or Karma, can be avoided or at least controlled by human effort. The age of dogmas is fast dying away and an age of scientific questioning has set in. In Europe and America, God and the Church are being replaced by modern science. Russia is trying to banish both. Germany has substituted the Führer and the Fatherland. The democratic countries just tolerate them. But in all countries old beliefs are rapidly falling away, to give place to new, and religion itself is taking the shape of what may be called Scientific Humanism.

True, this is substituting one illusion for another. True, again, man cannot live without illusions. But the point is, our illusions must change according to changing times lest they degenerate into harmful ones incompatible with the changed conditions of society. Nor should they be allowed to remain, lest the saner half of the people lose faith in intelligence and the other half live in comparative superstition.

Women and Marriage in India

Since the Vedas and the Puranas are unable to stop the motion of the sun, the moon, and the earth, they are inadequate to supply the ethical needs of all times. Humanity is always changing and its codes of ethics must move in pace with these changes. The values of the ancients have little meaning for us moderns, as the necessity which called their laws and institutions into being has long since disappeared. The taboo prohibiting sea voyages, for example, might have originated in a seafaring age when migration to Java and other islands depopulated Aryavartha; but it has no meaning for us to-day, when our problem is over-population and not under-population. Drinking Ganges water might have been forced on ancient Aryans as a religious duty when pure water was scarce and migration from the Punjab had to take place along the branches of rivers; but with our modern methods of purifying water, it is criminal to ask people to drink the filthy water near Benares as a religious duty. Pilgrimages were invented to make people travel at a time when roads were unsafe and people reluctant to undertake the hazards of long journeys without promises of eternal rewards; but to tell an Indian of to-day that a journey to the stench-ridden city of Benares is more elevating to the soul than a trip to Kashmere is to confess to a lack of aesthetic sense. The worship of the cow was, perhaps, a virtue in an age when agriculture was laborious and people had to be compelled to abandon their old, lazy habit of killing cattle and eating the meat; but cow-worship is degrading to the dignity of a twentieth-century human being.

However much we might revere our ancestors as pioneers

Wanted: New Values

of civilization, we cannot accept their standards as binding on us. Whatever be the lofty pretensions of our ancient literature as embodying eternal wisdom, in the light of the accumulated wisdom of all nations all down the ages which we are now heirs to, the outlook of our ancestors was tribal. The laws expressly framed for a few Aryans who lived in the land bounded by the Vindhya and the Himalayas (Manu says his law obtained only in Aryavartha) cannot be accepted by us as universally binding or infallible.

A belief in the infallibility of the ancient texts gives us an entirely misleading idea about the past. It makes us go backward. To the generality of believers, the miracles and signs mentioned in the texts are miracles and signs pure and simple, and they are convinced that in those days gods were in the habit of holding free converse with mortals. People there are among us (not peasants and labourers, but men and women well-educated as our standards go) who believe that Hanuman, by the power he obtained through devotion and Brahmacharya, jumped over the Gulf of Mannar, and that Kumbhakarna's moustaches were three hundred yards long, because in the golden age such things were possible. Europeans who smile at the credulity of the superstitious Hindu would do well to remember that there are millions of apparently sane Europeans who believe that in the year A.D. 33 Jesus was crucified and buried, rose from his sepulchre after three days and after spending forty days with his friends ascended to heaven in the corporeal body; that in still earlier times God used to give personal instructions to the Jews through their leaders how to conduct their foreign policy; and that an ass spoke good Hebrew. In fairness to the faithful, it may be added that the illusion of time has found favour with some evolutionists, too, who have developed a tendency to explain the unknown by multiplying ages and talking of millions and millions of years.

Now, the free converse of gods with sages mentioned in the scriptures, whether Hindu or Hebrew, was mostly the invention of those who made the populace observe the laws by inspiring awe in them, as the police was not sufficient for this in those remote days. Moreover, science was in its infancy, the world was not mapped, physical phenomena were attributed to supernatural agency, people knew very little about their neighbours (let alone about distant nations) and conditions were generally such that men and women were willing to believe anything if it were said loudly enough. If some Phoenician Sinbad wandered through unknown lands and got back with a couple of sailors' yarns about men with one eye and men whose heads grew under their shoulders his countrymen were all the more ready to believe him because nobody knew what strange beings inhabited the mysterious lands beyond the Pillars of Hercules. Ignorance about perfectly natural phenomena like eclipses, earthquakes, and meteors aided the ancients to invent miracles and the wrath of the gods. Then there were priests who knew a thing or two about physics and chemistry, and, keeping this knowledge to themselves, awed the people into submission by creating phantoms and apparitions.

If we, in the twentieth century, have a lesser number of miracles than in the Satyuga, it is not because we are a degenerate race on whom the gods look with indifference, but because we know too much about gods and the ways of men to be easily duped.

It may be mentioned that we can find authority for almost

Wanted: New Values

anything in our ancient books which are considered infallible revelations. Polyandry and polygyny are sanctioned by the Vedas; the Aswins had only one wife between them and many Rishies had a plurality of wives. Thieving and gambling are permitted by the Vedas; there are Mantras expressly written for success in these activities. Drinking was a religious duty for Vedic Aryans. There are hymns that can be quoted in defence of and against the caste system. There is Vedic sanction for beef-eating and, according to Rajendra Lala Mitra, even for human sacrifice. Those who believe in a personal god as well as the Vedantist and the follower of the atheistic Sankya system, swear by the Vedas. The Sanathanist defends idolatory and the Arya Samajist denounces it, both on the authority of the Vedas.

As for the Puranas we can quote their sanction for any crime under the sun. Treachery, murder, obscenity, adultery, rape, illegitimacy, debauchery, sati, sadism, masturbation can all be proved to be sanctioned by the Puranas. I do not deny that there is besides much wisdom and kindliness, but I only maintain that the ancient texts cannot be taken as an infallible authority for human behaviour or morality. Of course, they had their uses in their own times, when India was in her infancy; but mature India should have little use for them except for antiquarian interest.

However comforting the theory that we have the sanction of antiquity for all our progressive movements might be for those pious people who fear a sin in every deviation from traditional usages, truth compels us to admit that our progressive movements are not the result of better enlightenment as to the meaning of the ancient texts. The breakdown of the caste system is not, for example, inspired by our knowledge that in early Vedic times there was no caste, but is rather the result of the increased enlightenment of Hindus as to the injustice of the institution, aided no doubt by their contact with Muslims and Christians and by the demand of educated Harijans to be treated as human beings. The Sarda Act, too, was not prompted by the study of the Vedas and a realization that the mention of child-marriage is absent from the Vedas, but rather by a consciousness of its iniquity that developed among enlightened Indians. It is not the ancient text that drives us forward, but rather our own innate desire for improvement, influenced doubtless by environmental factors. Ancient texts are revered not for their wisdom but for their grey hairs.

Ancient Indians, we are asked to believe, were a highly cultured race with edifying codes of love, peace, and good will to others. Innumerable quotations from Vidura, Vyasa, and other sages are given to illustrate this point. But a careful scrutiny of the texts would reveal to us that these teachings were seldom comprehensive of all humanity. The Vedas, like the Old Testament, preach the ruthless destruction of enemies. Some of the Puranas, in spite of their confusion, show more tolerance, as by the Puranic times many non-Aryan elements had entered the Hindu fold. Anyway, the doctrines of Pacificism and Ahimsa preached by certain sages always remained in the palm-leaves, and if there were pacifists of the type of Yudhishtir, who longed for peace at any price, there were militants like Krishna who preached the philosophy of extermination, and these, as usual, prevailed over the pacifists. And if, in the Mahabharata War, they did not fight with poison gas and bombs, it was not because the ancients had better ethics than we ourselves have, but

Wanted: New Values

because their worst weapons were arrows and clubs; it also remains to be proved that Bhima's method of ripping open Dussasana's belly, making a garland of his entrails, and drinking his blood, is a more humane way of killing an enemy than dropping a bomb on him.

The ancients were in no way ethically more advanced than we. If they had their Sidhartha and Jesus, we have our Gandhi, Wells, Tagore, and Romain Rolland. And if these sages have lesser illusions than their predecessors, the advantage is ours.

It must be emphasized that India cannot afford to wait for reforms till all the elders are converted. Conventional people never consent to reforms. If reformers suffered themselves to be bullied by conventional people, society would have perished like the snake that could not slough its skin. It is futile to wait. We must remember that conventional people would not believe that the earth moved round the sun. They persecuted Copernicus for revealing this fact: unable to move themselves, they were incapable of grasping the idea of a mobile earth.

But in spite of the conventional people, society moves, nevertheless. India moves and is determined to move. We, too, have entered an age of revolt and have broken many a convention. We have pulled down the priest from his pedestal and have held him up to ridicule. We have broken the heads of our idols. We have smashed the barriers of caste, the very foundation of Hindu society. We have dragged down the scriptures from their Olympian heights and have given them over to the Sudra and the Panchama. We have passed the Sarda Act in spite of Manu and Parasara. We cross the black waters with impunity and tell the objectors to go to hell. We laugh at our princes who are descended from the sun and the moon. We touch untouchables and eat before washing. Why, we have even learnt to bully God's Englishmen.

But this is not enough; it is only the beginning. With the exception of a few enlightened people who work for the salvation of our country, India still lies buried in medieval squalor, and Manu still rules. The Caliphate, driven out of Arabia, Egypt, and Turkey, sits enthroned among the Indian Muslims. Women in India are still personal property; they have not yet received recognition of their individuality. A woman cannot be called by her proper name but by such vague terms as "the family," "the home," or the Zenana of such and such a man. Higher education for women is condemned on moral and hygienic grounds. Independent paid work is for them considered degrading. Nursing, midwifery, and stenography are classed as forms of prostitution, good enough for Anglo-Indians and Indian Christians. Child-marriage flourishes in spite of the Sarda Act. Girls who go for evening strolls, sea-bathing, boating or playing, who dress with taste or do anything that enhances their health and good looks, are loudly condemned from the pulpit and the platform as degenerate imitators of cheap Westernism. And, to crown all, we have still to tolerate the sight of poor innocent women hobbling along the street in stiffling, filthy, verminous veils.

In most of our native states antediluvian laws are administered by medieval tyrants. The tyrants of the medieval days, it must be remembered, had to behave themselves to a certain extent for fear of the foreign invader and the internal trouble-maker, and the subjects of a despot never hesitated

Wanted: New Values

to use a dagger to remove a tyrant. But now the Englishman would let none of these things stand between a prince and his pleasure. The Sarda Act does not reach native states and the Rajah and the Nabob still live in medieval style with harems of sultanic scale. When veiled women tire them, they go to exploit the possibilities of London and Paris. Laws restricting traffic in women and children are not likely to be enforced with any vigour in a state the head of which himself stands in need of slave-girls, cup-bearers, and palace dancers.

These things must go. India must be made a country fit for civilized people to live in. Until recently, we could attribute all our miseries to the iniquity of the Britisher. But however much we might regret it, he is day by day making it increasingly difficult for us to make a decent complaint against him. We have ourselves to shoulder our responsibilities, let us do so without complaint.

SEX IN EDUCATION

Time there was when the written word was considered taboo for the common man, and even for kings and the nobility. Only priests were supposed to be competent to handle it. Slowly, however, the use of letters began to spread and the priest, no more able to check it, made a desperate attempt to save the law book and the scripture on which his authority rested, from the ravages of the mob. (The Catholic clergy in the Western world, it will be recalled, withheld the Bible from the laity.) The Vedas were the sacred property of the Brahmins and the Sudra who dared probe into its mysteries suffered mutilation or death. But the priest could not keep the scripture from the people for ever. In time the sacred texts became public property and to-day anyone who has the money to buy can read the Vedas and the Bible provided he has the patience to do so.

Although all the sacredness and mystery that once surrounded knowledge in general have fallen, there is still one branch of knowledge which is considered dangerous for the common man. It is sex. In spite of the fact that all men and women are born of the sex-act and all indulge in it, yet useful knowledge about it is condemned as sinful. And this hypocrisy is considered all the more necessary because of the desirability of keeping children and adolescents from premature sex-experience.

The necessity of keeping children and adolescents from premature sex-experience is recognized by all. But the present method of pretending to believe that the youngsters grow in purity and innocence when we tell them nothing about sex, far from serving any useful purpose, is doing untold harm to their health and morals. Ignoring a problem is no solution of it. Instincts, if ignored, are sure to run riot. Boys and girls have a right to know the functions of their organs and if their curiosity is not satisfied in the proper way they will satisfy it in improper ways. If parents and teachers refuse to take them into their confidence, young persons will seek knowledge elsewhere and become instructed in vice rather than in wisdom. This may be responsible for the widespread practice of homo-sexuality and onanism among boys and girls, for what else can be expected of youngsters who pick up their sex education from cheap advertisements, writing on the walls of latrines, and from

Wanted: New Values

older boys and girls already confirmed in vicious thoughts and acts?

Bertrand Russell, writing on the necessity of instruction to children on sex matters, observes:

"The fact that a mystery is made about sex enormously increases the natural curiosity of the young on the subject. If adults treat sex exactly as they treat any other subject giving the child just as much information as he desires or can understand, the child never arrives at the notion of obscenity, for this notion depends upon the belief that certain topics should not be mentioned. Sexual curiosity, like every other kind, dies down when it is satisfied. Therefore, far the best way to prevent young people from being obsessed with sex is to tell them just as much about it as they care to know.

"In saying this, I am not arguing *a priori*, but on the basis of experience. What I have observed among the children in my school has shown conclusively to my mind, the correctness of the view that nastiness in children is the result of prudery in adults. My own two children (a boy aged seven and a girl aged five) have never been taught that there is anything peculiar either about sex or about excretion and have so far been shielded to the utmost possible extent from all knowledge of the idea of decency with its correlative indecency. They have shown a natural and healthy interest in the subject of where babies come from but not so much as in engines and railways. Nor have they shown any tendency to dwell upon such topics either in the absence or in the presence of grown-up people. With regard to the other children of the school, we have found that if they came to us at the age of two or three or even four, they developed exactly like our children: those, however, who came to us at the age of six or seven had already been taught to regard anything connected with the sexual organs as improper. They were surprised to find that in the school such matters were spoken of in the same tone of voice as was employed about anything else and for some time they enjoyed a sense of release in conversation which they felt to be indecent; finding, however, that the grown-ups did nothing to check such conversation, they gradually wearied of them and became as clean-minded as those who had never been taught decency. They now get merely bored when children new to the school attempt to start conversation which they fondly believe to be improper. Thus, letting fresh air on the subject, it has become disinfected and the noxious germs it breeds when kept in darkness have been dissipated. I do not believe that it is possible by any other method to get a group of children whose attitude towards subjects usually considered improper is so wholesome and decent."*

The only thing we can do to prevent premature sex-indulgence and perverse practices among boys and girls is to enlighten them on the whole subject. Knowledge, no doubt, has its dangers. But it is not so dangerous as ignorance. If, for example, we teach a man the proper use of a gun he might be able to use it against us or himself with better aim. With all that, we know a gun is more safe with a person who knows how to use it than with one who knows nothing about it. The same may be said of sex, too. Every boy and girl is born with this metaphorical gun; and the fear of commiting suicide with better efficiency should not stop us from instructing the possessor in its proper use.

* Bertrand Russell: *Marriage and Morals* (George Allen & Unwin Ltd.).

Wanted: New Values

As children grow up, their knowledge about sex-matters must be increased to meet the curiosities and urges of coming adolescence. At present our boys and girls are so ignorant of these matters that when Nature produces in them the first signs of maturity, they are often cowed with shame. They dare not speak of it to parents, to whom questions on sex-matters are to be punished peremptorily. It is possible that they have not been altogether blameless in sexual matters and who could tell that this new development of shame is not the result of some misbehaviour? They may feel that they have been exceptionally wicked, and so they live under a nervous strain till they are relieved by information volunteered by a kind friend or an elderly relative.

Most of our boys and girls know little about sex except its various perversities and the consequence is that when they are married they seldom know what it is all about. They have a vague feeling, before marriage, that the nuptial night is going to be an embarrassing one, and the whispered instructions of old crones increase their terror. Cases have come to light of couples wedded for years who did not know how to perform the sex-act. Friends of mine have believed kissing to cause pregnancy, and I know of a girl, educated in a convent who, loving a young man, was afraid to indulge in pleasurable thoughts about him lest she conceive.

This appalling ignorance, however, obtains only among youngsters from conventional homes of villages and small towns and under the vigilance of jealous guardians. In the cities children know a thing or two about sex, especially about its shadier aspects. While the children of the upper classes pick up their forbidden knowledge from pictures, cheap books, from other children, and from servants, those of the poor and the lower middle classes get it from their parents and neighbours. The housing conditions of the city are such that among the lower classes children have to sleep in the same room as their parents, but it should not be supposed that children always sleep as soundly as they ought, leaving the parents to do what they like on the adjacent bed. At first, children become witnesses to their parents' behaviour by chance; but once the parents are caught in the act, the little ones begin to take an interest in these nocturnal activities. They even pretend slumber and remain awake to watch. And a child that has watched its parents (almost all children watch their parents without the parents themselves knowing) cannot but be impressed by the double morality of adults who practise at night what they condemn in the day. It is not likely that children would take these nocturnal sinners seriously although they might obey them for fear of the rod.

The sex hypocrisy of the parents gives rise to a morality in children by which there is no objection to sexual pleasures so long as they are indulged without the knowledge of adults. They begin to look upon secret sex-indulgence as a legitimate form of pleasure but its detection as shameful. This tends to establish a convention among children that they should indulge in sex as soon as opportunity arises without the chance of detection. And the reason why boys and girls left without parents or other adults have an inevitable tendency to abuses is not far to seek.

Throughout the ages moralists have deplored the perverse sex-life of the young and have sought redress in external restraints, in keeping young people in ignorance about their sexual organs and in using the rod mercilessly. As late as the eighteenth century, infibulation was preached as a remedy.

Wanted: New Values

A writer of this century, after enumerating a number of methods for preventing self-abuse among the degenerated youth of his time, says:

"All these means are sometimes not sufficient to damp the devilish fire of passion which when it bursts forth in full fury so inflames the natural instincts as to lead direct to onanism. All warnings, all vivid stories of death, the devil, and eternal damnation are lost upon the soul of such a slave of lust, just as a drop of water upon a glowing coal. How shall we meet this unspeakable misery? There is one way, which I indeed do not know from personal experience but which witnesses declare to meet with the desired result and which I advise urgently in doubtful cases. That method is infibulation."*

In this century of ours, none of us, not even the moralists, believe in infibulation as a remedy for onanism. We have discovered that the fire of passion, of which the medieval moralist writes with such feelings, is not so much a manifestation of the innate perversity of youth as of its resistance to unnatural restraints. A removal of these restraints and a belief in the good sense of youth would cool the fire appreciably.

Moreover, modern authorities tell us that mild masturbation, far from leading to lunacy or emaciation as is generally believed, is conducive to good health in the unmarried. They find the evil not in the act itself but in the sense of shame and fear of detection attached to it. Even homosexuality in their opinion is not so much an unnatural vice as a biological variation.

Be that as it may, there can be no two opinions about

* Dingwall: *Male Infibulation.*

the evil as it is practised in our schools and colleges. There may be some to whom homosexuality may not be unnatural or even may be normal, but to the large majority of people it is unnatural and undesirable. Even the fact that many of the famous men of history have been homosexuals does not modify the truth of this statement. In our present system of sex segregation, the abnormals are everywhere mixed with the normals; and the vices learnt in youth are hard to overcome.

In sexual matters the line that divides virtue and vice is thin. We have seen that there have been times when amongst certain nations sodomy was considered fashionable among the upper classes. It cannot be supposed that all who practised it were biological defectives. In fact, the morality that obtains among a people has a tendency to shape their attitude towards sex in that direction and unnatural practices can be easily made to look natural by regarding as fashionable or conventional. All those Greek and Persian poets who addressed their love songs to their own sex were not abnormals; their bad taste merely reveals the standard of morality of the times.

Thus it is imperative that we check the present tendency of drift towards a convention among youngsters that heterosexuality is a crime and homosexuality and autoeroticism legitimate forms of sex expression so long as they are practised without being detected by teachers and other guardians.

With the present taboos, parents and teachers would find it extremely embarrassing to instruct children and adolescents in sexual matters. Boys and girls who seek enlightenment would find it even more embarrassing. But a beginning has to be made sometime and the earlier it is made the better. After all, there is nothing particularly shameful about sex. We are all born of it, every one of us has sexual organs and,

Wanted: New Values

with negligible exceptions, all of us indulge in sexual intercourse at some time of our lives.

It is not known how we managed to collect so much shame around anything so common and of such everyday indulgence. Clothes perhaps have been the mother of shame. Although we are led to imagine that we wear clothes to cover our shame, there is every reason to believe that clothes gave birth to shame. Communities that developed in torrid zones without the necessity for clothing exhibit very little shame, especially those who have not been infected with the semitic epidemic of decency. In South India, for example, shame generally begins, as with Gandhiji, at the loins and ends at the knees; women there, particularly in Malabar, go about barebosomed and bareheaded. Among certain hill-tribes and fishermen of India the males wear only narrow pieces of cloth like fibulae about their private parts, thus reducing the area of their shame to a few square inches. Some African tribes are on a still higher plane of evolution. They wear nothing at all. The missionaries who blushed to look at these savages in the nude wanted to clothe them. But the savages were not instructed properly as to the particular parts where shame obtained and the next day came to the mission with only their heads dressed in militant finery.

Even among communities full of shame, the feeling is not at all absolute but varies with place and time. In beaches and riversides, people have little shame. In their bedrooms, men and women are revoltingly shameless. In railway carriages and religious processions people set aside many of their standards. Nor do we object to a male doctor entering the confinement chamber on the principle that it is immodest for a male to look at a female in the nude.

All of which shows that our ideas of shame are relative and that they are ruled by conventions and traditions. If we take courage and act, if we instruct our youths in sex just as we instruct them in other matters, very soon a convention will be set up which would look upon those who treat sex as a mystery as reactionaries.

That youth is entitled to some sort of knowledge in sex-matters is even now recognized, as is shown by the instruction imparted to young people on the eve of their nuptials by old crones. But there is no point in letting young men and women ruin health and morals throughout childhood and adolescence by ignorance. Nor does an hour's instruction exhaust the subject. If the instructors knew what they were talking about even this would be of some value. But the knowledge of the crones is generally confined to superstition and they succeed only in frightening the young people, already nervous, out of all their wits. The instruction itself is a culminating point in hypocrisy, which makes us pretend that the young people remain innocent and pure in sexual matters till the eve of matrimony.

It is time we rid ourselves of this humbug and confessed that sex is part and parcel of the life of men and women, that it is an ever present problem and as much knowledge of it as can be digested is essential for our healthy growth from childhood onwards.

MOTHERHOOD

It has become a habit with us to talk exaltedly of motherhood, its nobility, its sweetness, and its preciousness, but there we leave it. The result is that in India motherhood has become a

Wanted: New Values

positive nuisance. The whole country is infested with swarms of mothers who breed in the street, on the banks of the Ganges, in huts, hovels, and sub-human homes. Nobody can cross an Indian street without being accosted by half a dozen beggar women who exhort charity on the strength of having given birth to half-dead babes whom they exhibit in their arms.

Leaving beggar mothers and shameless women aside, if we examine our normal mothers we would find that most of them are mothers because they couldn't help themselves. There is no will behind their motherhood. They mate because they are forced to do so by convention; they bear because they cannot avoid it; and they give birth to ease themselves. The whole process is a drift to fatal ruin.

We must get into our heads that there is no nobility or virtue simply in a woman being a mother. Any woman can be a mother even without marriage if she be reckless enough. Motherhood, to deserve admiration, should be wilful, responsible, and dignified.

To leave motherhood to take care of itself, and to expect healthy children and desirable citizens as a result, is like leaving the Indus to flow as it likes and hoping to find beautiful rice fields and orchards growing upon its banks. Unlike animals, human beings cannot be trusted to reproduce the race according to instinct. The instinct of *homo sapiens* is much impaired by reason and it is on the happy harmony of those two conflicting factors that the salvation of humanity depends. Centuries of life in artificial surroundings have confused our animal instincts and these have become un-trustworthy. The beasts of the field and the birds of the air know instinctively how to rear their young and to separate from them when they are able to care for themselves. But humans are still at a loss to find out an ideal solution to the question of rearing. The young of animals and birds are well fed by their parents and seldom starve for want of food, whereas the young ones of *homo sapiens* die in thousands from under-nourishment, neglect, and ignorance. All this shows that instinctive motherhood is not common to human beings and that human beings require to be trained to responsible motherhood. But no mere bookish training is indicated which, by the time a girl masters all the rules for radiant motherhood, lands her in the tuberculosis hospital.

The first qualification for motherhood should be physical fitness. We want our mothers to be healthy not only for the children's sake but for their own sake as well. For this our present-day ideas of modesty should undergo a radical change. The subject of women's health and the necessity of discarding our perverted standards of modesty have been discussed in a former chapter and need not be repeated here.

By far the most important part of the education for motherhood should be the care of children. For this a complete change in our ideal of womanhood is necessary. Hitherto, the education of women has been to make of them ideal wives. Devotion to the husband, implicit obedience to him in all matters, and the surrender of everything to his slightest whim, have been the qualities required of the perfect woman. And Sita embodies all these virtues. Sita must have been ideal at the time the Ramayana was written. It was a time when men were engaged in the pleasant job of reducing women to the status of slaves and toys, and they must have very well appreciated the actions of Sita in jumping into the fire at the whimsical command of her husband. But for New

Wanted: New Values

India we do not want such Sitas. We want our women to be reasonable human beings, with a sense of independence and a contempt of such superstitions as husband-worship and Linga-pooja. We must lay greater stress on motherhood than on wifehood. And motherhood means bearing and rearing children and nothing else.

The most delicate and important part of a human being's life is spent in the mother's womb and negligence at this period of one's life is likely to damage one's later life beyond hope. Yet, due to the senseless taboos attached to sex, this is the most neglected part of a person's life. We leave the happenings in the womb to Prajapati and think that everything is bound to be all right if a man doesn't tell his neighbours that his wife is pregnant. The woman herself knows little about her condition except that she is becoming more and more uncomfortable. In the case of the first child the girl is cowed by unknown terrors.

The result is a world of misery; and what is worse, miscarriages, painful births, maternal mortality, and infant mortality at the time of delivery, idiots, torn uteri, wreckage of the mother's health, and the hundred and one tragedies that result from this ignorance of the average woman about pregnancy and motherhood, are all accepted as the normal condition of the evil that is life.

A woman's life need not necessarily be so miserable as this. If we rid ourselves of our superstitions about sex, instruct ourselves in the vital process of reproduction, and make some effort to better our condition, most of these maternity tragedies can be avoided.

A. M. Ludovici has some interesting observations to make on the theory that it is natural for woman to bring forth her offspring in pain. In his opinion, the pain suffered by mothers is chiefly due to over-feeding in the period òf pregnancy, which makes the child abnormally fat and difficult to deliver. "The absurd superstition that a baby should be eight or nine pounds at birth is the root cause of the trouble," he says.

"Observing animals in a state of nature," he continues, "I arrived at this interesting conclusion, that their young, even when the mothers are in splendid fettle, are only skin and bone at birth, that their birth is an ecstatic function to the mother only when they are in this state and that young born in this way not only never lose weight but grow as plump and vigorous as could be wished in the first twenty-four hours.

"If, however, the gestating mother's food be so modified as to make it unlike the natural food of the species—for instance, if large quantities of potatoes, bread, cabbage, and rice pudding be given a female cat with rations of cooked instead of raw meat—the birth of kittens which are grossly fat is immensely difficult and some of them may be still-born or appear only after long delay in multilated fragments."

From this and various other observations he concludes that easing the pangs of childbirth is only a "question of ridding the public and the medical profession of a number of absurd prejudices."*

So much for the biblical curse that woman should bring forth her child in pain.

*　　　*　　　*　　　*　　　*

Although every woman should avoid bearing unwanted children, children once born should be taken proper care of.

* Ludovici: *Woman's Future and Future Woman.*

Wanted: New Values

It is doubtful if there is any country in the world where children suffer greater neglect than in India. In Japan, they say, every child is treated as a king or a queen. The Japanese show greater respect and civility towards children than towards adults. They never abuse or strike children. They wouldn't even say an unkind word to a child. Japanese children are loved like cherry blossoms.

How much of this is traveller's tale, I cannot say, as I have never been to Japan. In India, however, children are far from being as lovable and beautiful as cherry blossoms. It is seldom that one meets a healthy, lovable child in middle-class Indian society. The children one comes across in the street (the streets are the recognized playgrounds of children in the middle-class quarters of an Indian city) are generally dirty little creatures, tummies protruding, limbs tapering, and eyes tired. When they play, they seem to do it not for the love of games, but because they too seem to have caught up the convention that children should play. They have very little of the healthy wickedness of normal children, such as scaring dogs, hunting for birds and butterflies, and throwing stones at Sanyasies and madmen. I have seen many a child watch its comrades playing with the calm detachment of a minor Yogi.

If Indians cannot love such children it shows that they have not yet lost all aesthetic sense. The tendency of parents to beat children, to abuse them, to bully them, to chase them away when decent people are about and, finally, to send them away to school, should all be interpreted in this light, although all this is done for the ostentatious purpose of teaching children manners and discipline.

Children's ailments are so general in India that we have

Women and Marriage in India

come to believe that it is normal for children to be sickly. A healthy, cheerful child is taken as a freak and we suspect there is something wrong with it. We either under-feed our children or over-feed them. Many of them are let loose in the street to eat what they can get from hawkers of cheap bacteria-ridden foodstuffs. The parents themselves are not very strong in the matter of hygienic living and the children grow up in surroundings where decent men wouldn't let their dogs breed. The layout of the house, the shutting out of all air and light in the name of the Purdah, and the dumping up of all sorts of things in bedrooms and kitchens make the home of many a city dweller a veritable vermin-pit. All this produces constant ill-health among parents and children. When this is too chronic to be normal ill-health a doctor or an astrologer is consulted or God is prayed to. The latter remedy is generally found more attractive because it does not require any cash payment.

This is the lot of children bred in households with more children than are good for themselves or their parents. But there are other households wherein parents who have more money than is good for them beget an only child. In this case the child's fate is the worse. Since the parents are incapable of producing any more children they develop an exaggerated idea of the importance of the one and only, and incidentally of themselves. The child is believed to be a prodigy and its behaviour reminds the parents of the vagaries of Krishna, the courage of Shivaji, or the music of Tansen. If it smiles like an idiot, it is going to be a great wit. The mother gets jealous of her husband when the child shows any preference towards him. This gentleman, on the other hand, to make a man of him, teaches the child to abuse or beat its mother.

Wanted: New Values

Both love the child dearly and they dare not trust it to servants. They dare not send it out-of-doors because Mr. Henry Ford has built cars specially to run over it. If the child catches a slight cold, half a dozen doctors dance attendance upon it. If doctors fail to kill the child, astrologers are consulted. And they pay them well, too. And the child, after resisting all these persecutions as long as possible, dies one fine morning, leaving the parents sunk in sorrow.

This sort of imbecile parenthood is more damaging to children than neglect. A neglected child has at least the advantage of developing many spontaneous qualities in the fight from the cradle upwards. True many children might succumb to the adverse conditions. But those who survive are likely to be strong. A spoilt child, on the contrary, if it survives the mothering, is likely to develop into a moron. He will grow up, supposing the child is male, to be an egoist, a coward, or an ill-tempered philosopher. Under no circumstances will he be able to face the stern realities of life.

While proper education, however, can improve sentimental motherhood, no amount of education can improve the lot of neglected children when this neglect arises from their numerical unmanageability. A mother with, say, twelve children and a monthly income of about Rs. 40, is not likely to feed and clothe her children as she ought to, with all the education in the world. After twelve deliveries she wouldn't be healthy enough to look after herself let alone her children also. And the number of mothers who have gone through a dozen or more deliveries can be counted in India by the million.

Motherhood to be desirable should be wilful and voluntary and not accidental or forced. A child should not be accepted as an act of providence. With negligible exceptions every mother can have a child if she wants to and she need not have one if she doesn't want one. The barrenness generally found among the super-rich is not the result of God's curse on rich men (although our envy of their riches makes us fondly hope that it is so), but the result of Purdah, false modesty, and other static vices. Every normal woman is a potential mother. And in New India every woman should be able to judge for herself how many children are good for her and proceed to bear and rear them "according to plan." It is thus necessary that every girl of marriageable age should receive instruction in the most efficient method of practising

BIRTH-CONTROL

The Vedic cry of ten sons per mother does not hold good in modern India for the simple reason that our problem is not one of under-population but of over-population. Ancient Aryans, like the Hebrews, were a minority people, so to say, and they were in desperate need of manpower to fight against their numerous enemies and preserve their culture and religion. Moreover, they had ambitions of colonizing the whole of India and had to strain the bearing capacity of their women to the breaking point. We, in this Kali Yuga, have no such ambition. Our needs are but few. We want, on an average, say, three children per mother. We must learn to believe more in the quality of our children than in quantity.

Ever since the British made the martial virtues of Indians unmarketable, the various communities in India have been struggling hard to beat each other by sheer numbers. The proselytizing zeal of Christians, Muslims, and Arya Samagists

Wanted: New Values

actively aids this struggle. With the coming of representative institutions, based on communal electorates, the priest and the political pirate have embraced each other. There has started a mad rush for numbers in every community. The Indian Christian and the Muslim pull the Harijan by the hands, and the Hindu kicks him from behind into public wells and temples. There is a call to mothers not to think of birth-control while the other communities are alive. As the vote of every idiot is as good as that of a desirable citizen for all that the political pirate cares, he has come to think that an idiot is as good as a responsible citizen if he can but vote. This is one of the prices India is paying for premature democracy. But in spite of the worst efforts of Muslim communalists and Maha Sabhites, there is a growing tendency among the youth of the country, both Hindu and Muslim, to support the Congress and get less communalistic and more communistic.

India growing democratic, every adult male and female is likely to get a vote and it is for us to see that we would be much better ruled by the wisdom of a fewer people than the enormous stupidity of something like thirty-five crores of ignorami. But we cannot disinherit any of our countrymen, for this would lead to gross abuses of the type that obtains at present, namely, measuring the wisdom of a person by the revenue he pays to the State, which would reduce democracy to a farce. All we can do is to reduce the population to such proportions as would enable us to educate them and make them responsible citizens.

We must first of all rid ourselves of the craze for numbers. Throughout history it will be found that a well-disciplined and devoted minority always had the advantage over a loose and unorganized majority. Alexander with a handful of Greeks bullied the whole world. A few Romans, and later the Arabs, changed the history of the world. The Mongols, who overran the world from Moscow to the Indus, from Damascus to Pekin, were not countless. "The countless hordes of Mongol barbarians" was a lie propagated by Muslim historians unwilling to admit that the Faithful were less skilled as fighters than the infidels. In fact, Ghengiz Khan and his generals were masters of strategy and very often had to fight against overwhelming odds. In India, though the Brahmins have been negligible numerically, they bullied kings and enslaved the whole population. The Jews without a country or a home are even now ruling the finances of the world and are the only people of whom Hitler is afraid. The members of the Communist Party in Russia do not number more than five per cent of the population. And do we not find that a handful of Englishmen to-day are ruling something like thirty-five crores of Indians?

The Malthusian dread of humanity perishing, of population continuously struggling with the means of subsistence and reducing itself to nothing, may be a false alarm. It may be that there are sound laws underlying the population problem which prevent the possibility of humanity dying of starvation created by over-population. As soon as population reaches a certain level there seems to be a tendency for the birth-rate to decline. Again, more people are capable of creating more food. And, with our ability to make synthetic foods, there is no likelihood of world's food supplies becoming exhausted. Nor should starvation among the poor be pointed out as a symptom of over-population. Starvation is generally the result of unequal distribution of wealth, and therefore of

Wanted: New Values

foodstuffs, due to an unsound economic system. When there are millions of men and women starving in India, we must know, there are crores of bags of wheat and rice rotting in the godowns of our Marwari traders. In the medieval times, too, when India was less populated, thousands used to die of famine and want. Even when our ancestors lived in the jungle, a few men and women to a whole forest, many of our hunting forefathers must have died of starvation.

With all this, however, there is no doubt that India is over-populated. In India an increase in population is not met with a proportionate increase in the production of foodstuffs by means of improved and modern agricultural methods. There are no planned and collective efforts at large-scale production. The individual peasant ploughs and sows as his ancestors did two thousand years ago, and there is acute shortage of food all over the country. If the import figures are not convincing, and even if there are exports of foodstuffs from India, it should not be taken as a sign of plenty, but as a reflection on the purchasing power of the peasant who is unable to get the necessaries of life without starving his family and selling the precious grain. And while there is a universal cry for land there is no land to be given to the peasants. All told, the producing power of the peasantry remains practically the same while the population goes up by leaps and bounds.

Apart from the food problem there are other things which make India an over-populated country. Our population is such that any reformer who tries to do something for India is staggered at the enormity of it. The question of compulsory education for the masses confounds him. The problem of creating political consciousness among them overwhelms him. Economic uplift of the masses baffles him. He stands helpless against the slums of the city and the pressure of the peasants against forests, hills, and pasturelands.

So none can deny that we would be a happier country if there were less of us. And that is reason enough for us to advocate birth-control. Some would point out that there are other peoples, like the Japanese who by their superior skill and energy manage to solve their population problem without resorting to birth-control. But Indians are hardly civilized enough to solve their problem by rifling the pockets of the poor Chinese.

In medieval India, Nature used to solve the population problem in her own wasteful, sluggish way. Famines broke out in places and men and women died like locusts. Cholera and smallpox took their toll of human lives. Hordes of raiders came down the Khyber, massacred as many Indians as their leisure permitted and went their ways with the women and children as slaves. But now these primitive controls of population are closed to us. Thanks to the railways our White masters have given us, we have no famines in India at present but an equal distribution of starvation. We do not allow cholera and smallpox to depopulate the land, but anticipate these maladies and inject into the people as much of the diseases as will keep them lingering without dying. As for the raiders and their massacres, the British do not permit the Persians, Afghans, or any but themselves to massacre us. And, since the days of the Mutiny, the massacres of the British have never been widespread and effective. Small massacres like the Jallianwala Bagh create nothing but a furious indignation in the hearts of the people.

Thus, all the primitive checks to population are ended, and the aim of this book is in any case against the tendency

Wanted: New Values

to let India drift towards her doom in the way of Nature. We have a will and we want to shape our destiny according to it. If there is over-population, we must find a means to bring it within desirable limits.

Again, apart from national problems, there are individual problems to be considered. One woman, no doubt, is capable of producing a large number of children. But there is a limit to the number she can bear without impairing her health and affecting the economic resources of her family. A woman who begins her motherhood at the age of, say, fourteen is theoretically capable of giving birth to about twenty children by the time she reaches the age of forty, supposing, for argument's sake, that she does not die in the meantime. But all of these twenty children, under present conditions, are not likely to survive their childhood and of those that do survive some are sure to end up in the street, asylum, or hospital. It is much better to have two or three children of good condition, which the mother can bear and rear conveniently, than twenty congenital idiots.

On the issue of limiting children to a manageable number there is universal agreement among all educated men and women. But it is over the means of achieving this end that opinions differ. Some condemn as sinful all forms of artificial birth-control; it is unnatural they say; they preach abstinence as the only form of birth-control that should be practised. They assume that since some people find it easy to abstain for any length of time, others also can do likewise. Some even further maintain that since the sex-act is itself a sin it can be only atoned for by accepting children as punishments.

It is true that artificial birth-control is unnatural. In that sense, however, the whole life of man from the cradle to the grave is unnatural. It is unnatural to wear clothes; it is unnatural to use motor cars and electric light. It is unnatural to cross the Atlantic in a liner, it being more natural to swim over. It is unnatural to shave; it is unnatural to read and write; and it is unnatural to take medicines. To close the natural check to population by the unnatural methods of innoculation against cholera and smallpox, and the distribution of food against famines, and then to object to artificial birth-control on the ground that it is unnatural is illogical. To feed our children on cooked food which have none of the cleansing properties of raw food and then to oppose their cleaning teeth on the ground that it is unnatural to use brush and paste, is, as Bertrand Russell points out, to court the practical possibility of stinking teeth in children. Partial naturalism, especially when misapplied, is a dangerous doctrine.

The Hindu moralist's ethical objection to artificial birth-control is not so much the result of the vague embryo-murder doctrines of the codes as the influence of the orthodox Christian Churches. The Christians' objection to birth-control seems to be based on an obscure passage in the Old Testament. It appears there was a Hebrew gentleman named Onan who, according to custom, was compelled to "go into" his widowed sister-in-law and raise seed to his dead brother. The idea seemed so repugnant to Onan that while performing his duty he "spilled it on the ground" thus defeating the very purpose for which he "went into" his sister-in-law. At this the Lord was wrathful and punished him, but it is still disputable whether the punishment was for the refusal to raise the required seed or for "spilling it" on the ground. The Roman Catholics and certain other orthodox Churches

Wanted: New Values

hold that it was for the latter that the Lord punished Onan; other churches think differently. The Roman Catholics themselves believe in the necessity of practising some sort of birth-control and they advise their followers to restrict intercourse to a certain "safe period" in which conception is less likely to take place, but most medical men consider that this so-called safe period is as much a myth as the season of women mentioned by Manu. The Protestants are less scrupulous in these things and practise birth-control with and without the permission of their clergy.

These varying standards of ethics that obtain in various Christian churches sometimes give rise to curious situations. I know a Roman Catholic girl who is married to a Protestant, and the couple solves its birth-control problem thus: the wife, being a pious Catholic, refuses to use any artificial appliances, but would restrict intercourse to the "safe period." Thus they continue intercourse within the safe period, the girl using no mechanical means, but the husband, who has the sanction of the Lambeth Conference to use rubber goods, using a sheath as an additional precaution.

An analysis of the objections of moralists will convince us that these are founded on no sounder authority than the old repugnance to sex. To the moralist, whether Hindu, Christian, or Muslim, sex itself is bad enough, and he simply cannot imagine people complicating it with pessaries, sheaths, and other appliances.

But there is also the hygienic objection to artificial birth-control. True, birth-control, as it is clandestinely practised in India to-day, is unhygienic and immoral. But the fault lies not with the methods of control but with the ignorance of those who practise it and the shame attached to it. Young men and women are not allowed to obtain clean and scientific knowledge of sex and birth-control, so that they gather their knowledge only from the advertisements of charlatans trading on public ignorance. Decent men and women may not read a book on sex except behind closed doors; no man or woman can go to a chemist to buy a condom or pessary without a sense of guilt and without endangering his or her reputation; and in these circumstances, if people use the wrong methods and get into difficulties, there is nothing for us to be surprised about. The only solution to the problem is free and unashamed instruction in scientific birth-control to all young men and women of marriageable age.

We know that in spite of all the hostility of the elders, the use of contraceptives in India is widespread. Hence, it is worth while that it should be practised properly, when it is not injurious to health. It is in any case not half so harmful to health as continence or excessive childbearing.

Lastly, there is the economic objection to birth-control. People tell us that birth-control appliances are too costly to be bought by the poor in India, who due to their prolific nature, stand more in need of birth-control than anybody else. If there are parents in India to whom a few condoms or pessaries are more expensive than children, it is very essential that such parents should not be allowed to bring any children into the world. But as a matter of fact, except among those who breed in the street, a child is very much more expensive than birth-control. Even among peasants and labourers a child consumes in a month double the amount of money required for buying birth-control appliances for a year. But there are, in fact, chemical preparations which can be made at home without much expense.

Wanted: New Values

Even supposing, for argument's sake, that there are in India people too poor to buy birth-control appliances, is that itself any argument against free instruction in birth-control? Because secondary education is costly in India, do we close our high schools? If the poor cannot practise birth-control, why deprive the rest of its advantages?

Again, in my opinion, birth-control is more essential among the middle class than among the peasantry and the proletariat. In a democratic country it is the middle class who have to wield power and it is to them that the country looks for help and guidance. The middle classes are at present all the more important because of the small numbers of the upper classes and the political disinheritance of the very poor. But, unfortunately, the middle classes in India are the most wretched of all the classes. It is the middle classes with their miserable moral codes, their unhealthy ways of living, their antideluvian conventions, and their unemployment problems that stand in urgent need of controlled, well-ordered life. Before we tackle the problem of the peasant and the mill-hand, we must deal with the half-educated Babu who is too proud to do manual work yet servile enough to slave in the city office. No middle-class family should have more than three children.

There is a genuine fear among the upper classes that if they practise birth-control and the lower classes do not, the latter would outbreed them and annihilate their culture. This fear is unwarranted. There are no hard and fast rules that define the classes in a modern community. With the peasants and labourers educating their children and with the breakdown of the barriers of caste, there is nothing to prevent a labourer's son becoming a merchant, a capitalist, or a *petit bourgeois* clerk. If the upper classes become fewer, rest assured the lower classes will step gradually and unnoticed into their places. In this commercial age, the classes are recognized by the wealth they possess, and poverty and riches are not inherited like syphillis, although our foolish laws of inheritance lead us to imagine they are. Class distinctions would change with corresponding changes in the law or in conventions.

In spite of the objections of the moralists, humanity has always practised artificial birth-control or population-control by some means or another. In ancient and medieval times, it generally took the form of infanticide. Till very recently, this practice was very common in India and there is reason to believe that it still lingers in many parts of the country. Polyandry served also to control population. Among many savages, crude methods of abortion are practised. Onan's method, mentioned elsewhere, though not sanctioned by Jehovah, is representative of the practice among the Jews.

Thus, whatever the commandments of the Almighty on the subject, mankind has always felt the necessity of restricting the growth of population, with or without the sanction of the Law. We must appreciate this genuine difficulty and solve the problem in a rational and humane fashion without allowing the views of the Almighty to interfere with the happiness of mankind. The scientific use of contraceptives is a humane and intelligent way of doing it.

A working knowledge of contraceptive methods among people of marriageable age would inevitably lead to the breakdown of contemporary Indian morality. That would be beneficial, too, for contemporary morality is badly tainted with medieval asceticism and superstition, and detrimental

•

Wanted: New Values

to the well-being of humanity. We want a morality which aims more at the happiness of mankind than the whim of an imaginary godhead. And for this new moral values are required. "When the point of view of the ennobling of the race has penetrated the ethical ideas of mankind, the following may be described as immoral with a force now unsuspected:

All parentage without love,
All irresponsible parentage,
All parentage of immature or degenerate persons,
All voluntary sterility of married people, and,
All such manifestations of sexual life as involves violence or seduction and entail unwillingness or incapacity to fulfil the mission of the race."*

With the spread of contraception, that double morality which ordains one standard for woman and another for man would naturally disappear. If men can be immoral without consequence, women, too, could do likewise. This would establish, to a certain extent, the equality of sexual rights.

I must again admit, there would be abuses. But fear of abuse should never be a criterion in judging the desirability of a useful change. Knowledge of birth-control is essential to every woman and if there is any woman who might abuse that knowledge so much the worse for her.

Closely connected with birth-control is the problem of

EUGENICS

While man takes particular care in the breeding of horses, dogs, and pigs it is a pity that he leaves his own species to breed as it likes. Much as we deplore this state of affairs

* Ellen Key.

to-day, we can do little. We do not know enough about our own species to form an accurate idea of what sort of people are likely to produce the most desirable types of children. When we try to draw conclusions from the parentage of outstanding men whom accident has thrown up, we find our helplessness all the more exasperating. Had it not been for Napoleon his parents would never have been heard of. Voltaire's parents possessed none of the qualities that distinguished him. In spite of the myths woven round Jesus, his parents must have been very ordinary human beings. So were Mohammed's. Gandhiji's parents were never famous for the qualities that distinguish their son, and his own sons have not as yet shown a genius similar to his. As a rule geniuses do not beget geniuses. That is one of the reasons why government by heredity failed. If Akbar knew how to beget sons like him, the Great Moghul would have been still ruling in Delhi.

Certain insects like the bees have perfected the science of positive eugenics and are able to produce the required number and quality of workers, drones, and queens. We know very little about their methods. If we put too much stress on the physical side in our selection of desirable breeders, there is some possibility of producing monsters without intellect. If on the other hand we concentrate on the intellectual side, we might produce a nation of ill-tempered, wrangling philosophers. Further, for obvious reasons, scientists cannot experiment eugenically with human beings as they can with animals. All that we know of positive eugenics is that normally healthy people under favourable conditions produce normally healthy children. The results of education and environments, too, might or might not

Wanted: New Values

agree with the product of the eugenist. All told, positive eugenics is a science in its infancy and the dream of the eugenist of a society in which scientists would produce the required types of politicians, poets, engineers, mathematicians, film-actresses, and so on is a long, long way off.

In the realm of negative eugenics, however, we are on surer ground. We know an unwanted person when we see one. We do not want lunatics, for example, among us. We do not want the babes of the street, starved to a skeleton by their beggar parents so as to strike pity in the beholder and extract charity from him. We do not want its parents either. We do not want the hordes of parasites that wander all over India in the name of Sanyas. Nor are we in need of lepers and decrepits. All these persons are unwanted; they have a degenerating effect on the whole population; they live by the work of honest men and women and in return give the country vermin, disease, crime, imbecility, filth, and a bad name. Yet these are the very people who have lost all sense of restraint and breed prolifically. Devoid of other pleasures and unable to take a healthy interest in the joys of living, they take to sex with reckless abandon. It is notorious that lepers and consumptives are more unrestrained than normal men. It is too much to expect continence and chastity out of lepers, madmen, and congenital idiots; yet it is imperative that they should not be allowed to reproduce their kind.

There are only two ways of preventing the undesirables contaminating the community and of stopping them from reproducing themselves. The rational method is to destroy them. But man does not live by reason alone. In spite of all our wars, massacres, communal riots, and legal hangings, we feel it is not right to take life when we can possibly help it. We recognize the right of every person to live and only those who refuse to recognize this right in their fellow-beings stand in danger of the scaffold. In other words, we do not hang a man unless he has committed a murder.

Even rationally, destruction of the unfit would be an unsound move. It would soon degenerate into destruction of the unprofitable, old men and women included. Further, when destruction of the unwanted is accepted in principle there would be plenty of captains of industry to persuade us to believe that the unemployed are unwanted, too.

The destruction of the unfit thus ruled out, the only alternative is their segregation and sterilization. The State should undertake the segregation and sterilization of lunatics and those afflicted with incurable maladies as a first step towards civilizing India.

Conclusion

★

INDIA is on the threshold of freedom. This is a time in the history of our country wherein we want healthy, virile men and women. We want them for the simple reason that we cannot stop an invading army by repeating Mantras from the Atharva Veda or by preaching the edifying doctrine of non-violence to the soldiery. As for the possibility of wars, the recent experiences of Abyssinia and China clearly show that the age is not yet past wherein strong nations prey upon the weak.

We cannot expect healthy, virile men and women to be born of child-wives, slave-mothers, and anaemic Purdah-nishins. For a free and healthy generation of Indians, we want free, healthy, mature mothers and fathers, and a family wherein parents live in peace and children are brought up properly. Above all, we must insist upon the physical and mental fitness of women for motherhood. It is in the womb of woman that great victories are won.

One thing is certain: unless our marriages and the home produce better Indians than to-day either our conventional marriages and home-life must go, or India. And since India is greater than the conventions, it is in the fitness of things that the conventions must go. And go they will. Everything points to that. While Malavya and the Pundits are thinking of holding conferences to discuss the desirability of intermarriage between the different Brahmin groups, young India is thinking in terms of companionate marriage and communism. The increasing number of young women who take the law into their own hands when parents fail to do fairly by them, the much-dreaded modern girl who refuses to reconcile herself to the degrading conditions of conventional marriage and so remains unmarried and deprives the country of desirable children, the popularity of films and novels that ridicule conventional morality, the eagerness with which Lindsey, Ellis, and other moral revolutionaries are read, are all symptoms of a healthy nation trying to shake off her fetters. Nobody need view these things with alarm. They merely show that India is not yet completely drained of her vital powers.

Tyrants, however, might create trouble. A nation with potential vitality cannot be oppressed beyond a certain point. History tells us of many political revolutions. There have been revolutions in morals, too; the license of the Restoration period in England brought about by Puritan tyranny was one of these. India is reaching the breaking point politically and socially. Only those short of vision can say that the India which has shed so much blood between the Mahabharata battle and the Sepoy Mutiny is incapable of spilling more. The shrewd Britisher knows it. That is why he is expanding the political scope of the country and avoiding an explosion. Tyrants of social codes, too, would be well advised to make a similar gesture. If they will not make marriage and the family bearable, the youth of India will break loose. Then woe to the sanctity of matrimony and the beauty of our home-life. But if such a thing happens, not only would the sanctity of matrimony and the so-called beauty of our home-life go,

Conclusion

but, as in all revolutions, the institutions themselves might go also. This is a calamity we must avoid. Just because we have bad laws, to break which, as Gandhiji has taught us, might be a virtue, it is not good that we should live without the law. So those who love the very desirable institutions of marriage and the family would do well to save them by making them fit for decent men and women to live in.

*   *   *   *   *

Some of our countrymen object to every progressive idea on the assumption that it is Western. The late Lala Lajpatrai was seriously troubled as to whether to class such persons as idiots or traitors. With me there is no hesitation: they are idiots and they are traitors—because they divide truth into East and West, and because they make progress in India very difficult if not actually impossible.

Are we to reject truth simply because it was discovered by a seer on the other side of Constantinople? Don't we know that Japan is to the west of us and America to the east if we go far enough? Are we to abandon travelling by train because a Westerner invented the steam engine? Are we to switch off the electric light and burn oil in defiance of Edison? Should we give up the motor car, the telegraph, and the aeroplane because we have no Vedic authority for these things? If we omit the West from our life, what have we got by way of the comforts we are used to? There are, of course, people who imagine that modern comforts are tortures; well, they may be for them. Nothing better can be expected of those who perpetually rail against life and its miseries.

We should not defer from borrowing anything from any

nation if it is good enough for us. In this we must follow the lead of the Japanese. Did the Europeans, by the way, hesitate to borrow religion from the Jews, art from the Greeks, medicine and astronomy from the Arabs, and the science of war from crusading Turks? If nations were foolish enough to refuse to learn from one another, is it possible the world would have made any appreciable progress?

India had been glutted with spiritual things for so long that to restore our balance it is essential that for a long while we think of little but our material welfare. And materialism, it must be remembered, is not exclusively Western. Patriots would note that we, in India, too, had our materialists. There was a time when the Charvakas and Nastikas disputed the authority of the texts with the leanest Rishi. Ajita Kesambalin, it is said, "resolved man into four elements which dispersed at death." Acharya Brihaspathi, most of whose Sutras were destroyed by orthodox Brahmins, has the following to his credit:

> There is no heaven, no final liberation nor any soul in another world.
> Nor do the actions of the four castes produce any real effect.
> The Agnihotra, the ascetic's three staves and smearing oneself with ashes,
> Were made by Nature as the livelihood of those destitute of knowledge and manliness.
> If a beast slain in Jyotishtoma rite will itself go to heaven,
> Why then does not the sacrificer forthwith offer his own father?

> While life remains, let a man live happily, let him feed on Ghee even if he runs into debts.
> When once the body becomes ashes how can it ever return again?

Conclusion

Hence it is only as a means of livelihood that Brahmins have
established here
All the ceremonies for the dead—there is no other fruit
anywhere.*

Brihaspathi has a thing or two to say about the Rishies
who composed the Vedas. "The authors of the Vedas," says
he, "were buffoons, knaves, and demons."

These Sutras of Brihaspathi contain doctrines Voltaire
would have envied. And the fact that Brihaspathi could not
prevail against the Brahmin conspiracy of his times is no
argument against the sanity of his doctrines. It is not always
truth that wins. The failure of Brihaspathi merely bears him
out as a genius born long before his times.

The material is as important as the spiritual, if not more
so. It is on the material that the spiritual rests. If we don't
believe in the material, all our talks about Swaraj, independence and economic uplift of the masses are meaningless.
These are symptoms of material hunger. And the fact that
India takes a keen interest in these things is proof enough
that, in spite of the dead weight of conventions, India is
passing from spiritual inertia to material activity.

* Quoted from *Sarvadarsanasamgraha*, by Sir Radha Krishnan, in
Indian Philosophy.

Index

★

Index

Women and Marriage in India

For Product Safety Concerns and Information please contact our EU
representative GPSR@taylorandfrancis.com
Taylor & Francis Verlag GmbH, Kaufingerstraße 24, 80331 München, Germany

www.ingramcontent.com/pod-product-compliance
Lightning Source LLC
Chambersburg PA
CBHW050433280326
41932CB00013BA/2091